Macmillan Junior Geography

③ **About the world**

Philip Sauvain

Macmillan Education

Introduction

The **Macmillan Junior Geography** series has been carefully graded to ensure that the level of the text, and the concepts introduced in each book, are written within the compass, grasp and experience of children of average ability aged 7–11 years.
Book One: How We Live has been written for average children aged 7–8 years;
Book Two: At Home and Around for 8–9 years;
Book Three: About the World for 9–10 years; and
Book Four: In Britain Now for 10–11 years.

All four books cover traditional subject areas, such as the major climatic and natural vegetation zones of the world, landforms, weather study, agriculture, industry and urban geography. At the same time, some of the concepts and techniques of the New Geography have been introduced wherever these are relevant and appropriate to the age and ability level of the pupils.

Many of the topics are covered in double-page units with assignments at the end of each section. The text has been designed in many cases so that it begins with an anecdote or some other means of immediately attracting the attention of the young reader.

It is hoped that the series will enable teachers to achieve a number of objectives when teaching geography to primary school age pupils. Children following this course successfully will commence secondary education or its equivalent in the middle school:

1. knowing something of the geography of their local area, having undertaken some simple fieldwork activities and local investigations.

2. knowing something of the main features of the human and physical geography of the British Isles.

3. knowing something of the geography of other parts of the world – including all the major climatic and natural vegetation regions, all the major forces shaping the land surface of the world, and some of the major world problems such as drought and irrigation.

4. having an elementary knowledge of basic skills and techniques in geography, such as those needed to record and display simple statistics, field sketching, learning from photographs and other sources of information.

5. having an elementary grounding in mapwork skills, which progress through the series from very simple beginnings in Book One.

6. having had some contact with the concepts and techniques of the New Geography – the analytical approach to the study of location and place.

Contents

Maps and plans — 4
Looking at a map — 4
Finding places on a map — 6
A plan drawn to scale — 8
Finding your way with a map — 10
Drawing a sketch map — 12
Using an atlas — 14
Looking at the globe — 16

Places where people live — 18
Living by a river — 18
Living in the mountains — 22
Living at the coast — 26
Living in a desert — 30
When a volcano erupts — 34
Living through an earthquake — 38

Rocks and soils — 40
About rocks — 40
About soils — 42
When soil blows away — 44

Water — 46
Storing water — 46
When rivers flood — 50

Forests — 52
From tree to paper — 52
Where elephants work — 54
Crops from trees — 56

Grasslands — 58
Land of tall grass — 58
Land of short grass — 60

Cold lands — 62
Life in the tundra — 62

Index & Acknowledgements — 64

Maps and plans

Looking at a map

A girl walks from her home to school. On her journey she crosses a bridge over a river, walks through a wood and passes two churches. One church has a square tower and the other a round spire, or steeple. She also goes past a telephone box and a post office.

We know this because we can see the journey she takes in the picture.
What are the first two things she sees after leaving home?
How many times does she have to cross a road on her way to school?

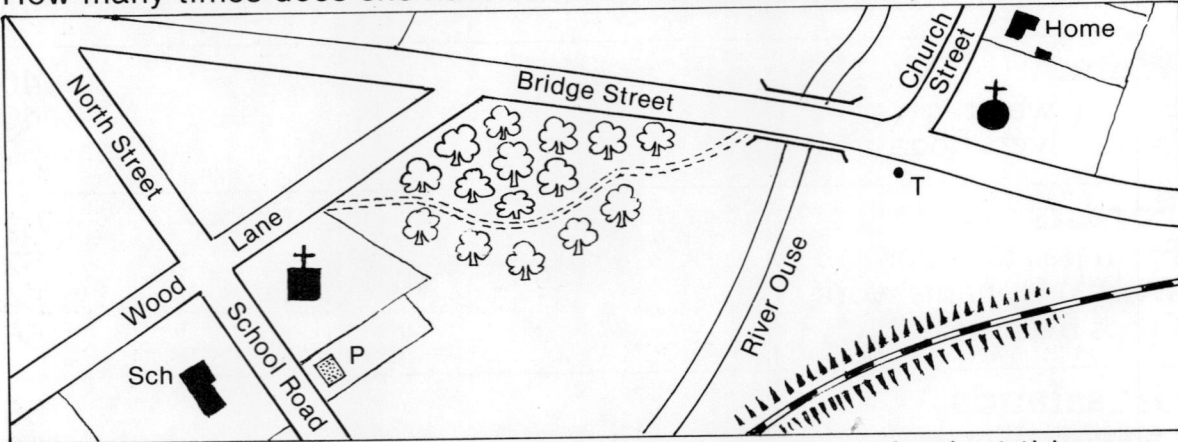

We can also see the same journey on the map above. Look at this map carefully. Then look at the picture again.
Where is the woodland? How is it shown on the map?
How can you tell from the map that one church has a square tower and the other church a round spire or steeple?
What streets does she walk down?

4

Small pictures and signs on a map, which stand for something, are called symbols.

Sometimes a small picture is used, like the trees which show where there is a wood. A sign is sometimes used, like the cross and the black square for a church with a tower. Sometimes buildings are just marked with a dot or a grey square, like the telephone box and the post office. The first letter in each word is printed alongside, such as 'T' for 'telephone' and 'P' for 'post office'. Letters which stand for a whole word are called abbreviations.

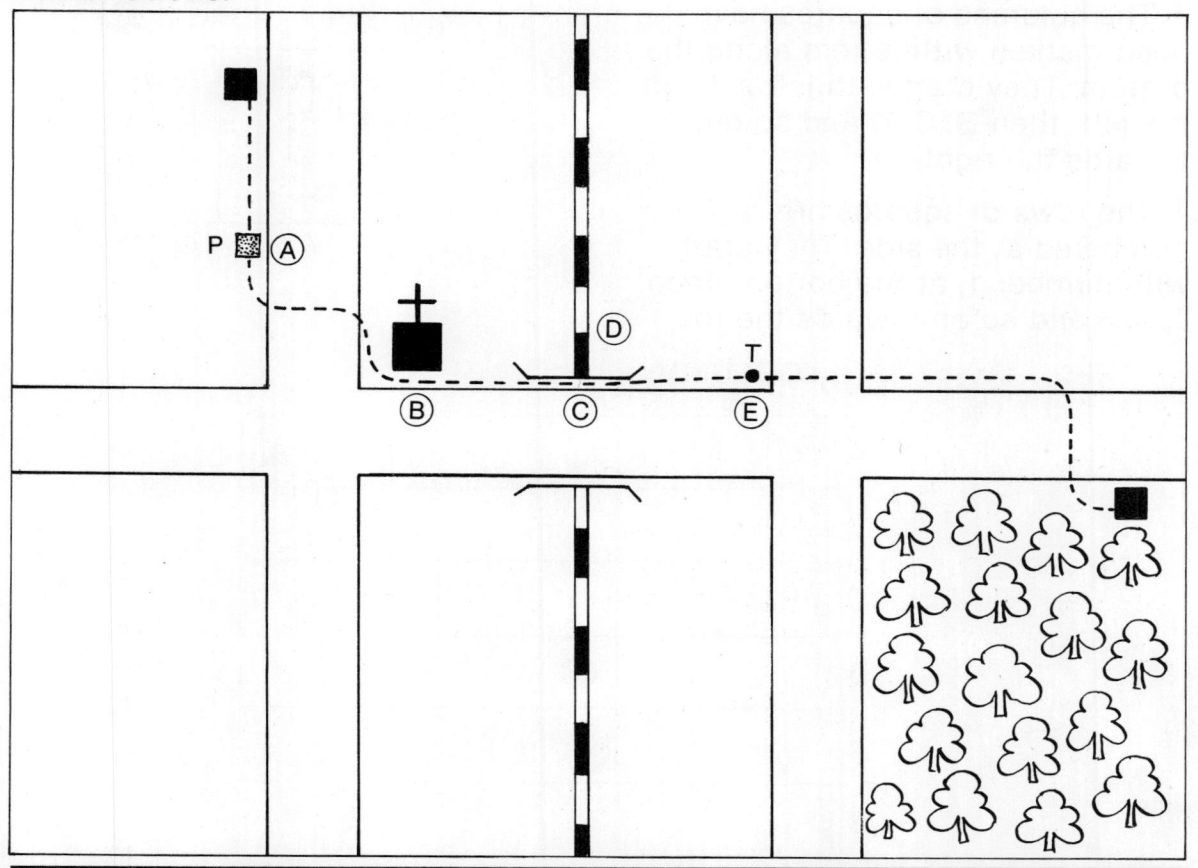

Things to do

1. If you saw the letters 'LB' near a post office what would you expect to see there?

2. How is the railway line shown on the map?

3. Look at the map on this page, showing the journey a boy makes when he leaves his home to play with a friend. Write down the names of the five things he passes lettered, A, B, C, D, E.

4. Features which are easily recognised are called landmarks. Can you think why?

5

Finding places on a map

Look at these squares. As you can see, each square has a letter and a number. If the girl is in A1, what square is the boy in?

Look at the squares below.

The columns of squares have been marked with letters along the bottom. They start with letter A, on the left, then B, C, D and so on towards the right.

The rows of squares are numbered at the side. They start with number 1, at the bottom, then 2, 3, 4 and so on towards the top.

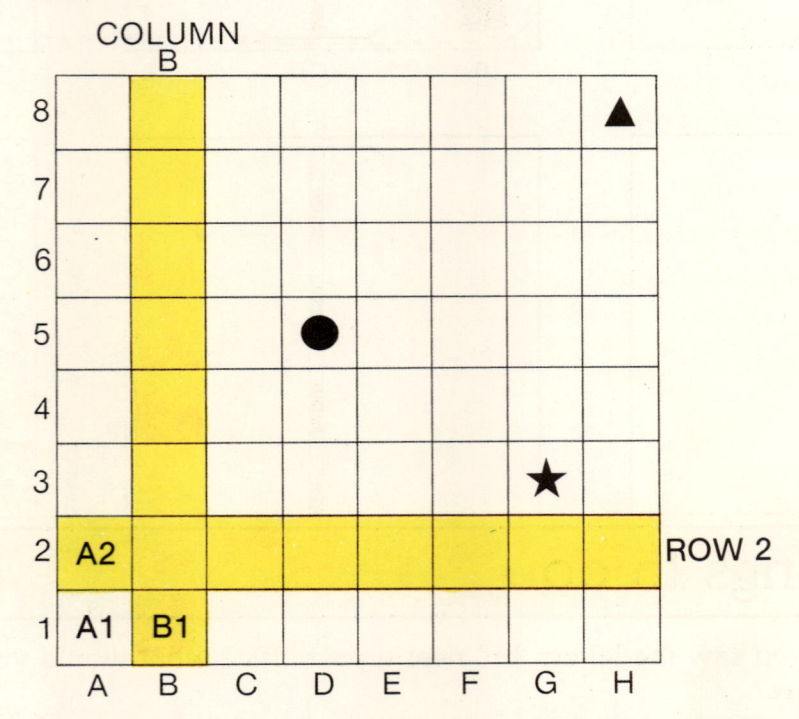

In this way each square can be given a different letter and number. It gets its letter from the column it is in, and its number from the row it is in. So the bottom left hand square is A1, and the square immediately above it, in the same column, is A2. The next square on the right of A1 is B1.

What are the letters and numbers of the squares which contain the circle, the triangle and the star?

6

Things to do

Look at the map on this page. As you can see, it has been divided into squares. The columns of squares are lettered A to N and the rows of squares are numbered from 1 to 10. So the church with a tower is in square E8. It is in the column lettered E and in the row numbered 8.

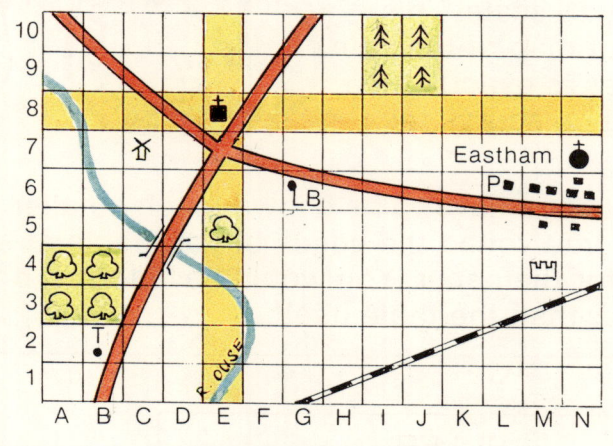

1. What can you see in squares G6, B6, E5 and K2?

2. In which square is
   1) the church with a steeple
   2) the post office
   3) the telephone box

3. What is the name of the feature in square E7?

4. In squares I10, I9, J10 and J9 you can see some pine trees. What symbol has been drawn to show these trees?

Windmill | Castle | Coniferous wood

5. Two other new symbols are shown on this map. You can see what they show in the pictures on this page.
   1) Write down their names and draw pictures of the symbols which show them on the map.
   2) What are the letters and numbers of the squares in which they are situated?

6. Draw symbols and write the abbreviations for three things you pass, or can see, on your way to school.

A plan drawn to scale

Put a coin on a piece of paper and draw round the edges.

This is one way of drawing a map of the coin exactly to scale. This means that on your map of the coin, the distance across is exactly the same as the distance across the coin itself.

On most maps things have to be shown much smaller than they really are. You couldn't draw round the edges of your table at school since it would be too big for the paper. You would have to make the map of the table much smaller than the table itself.

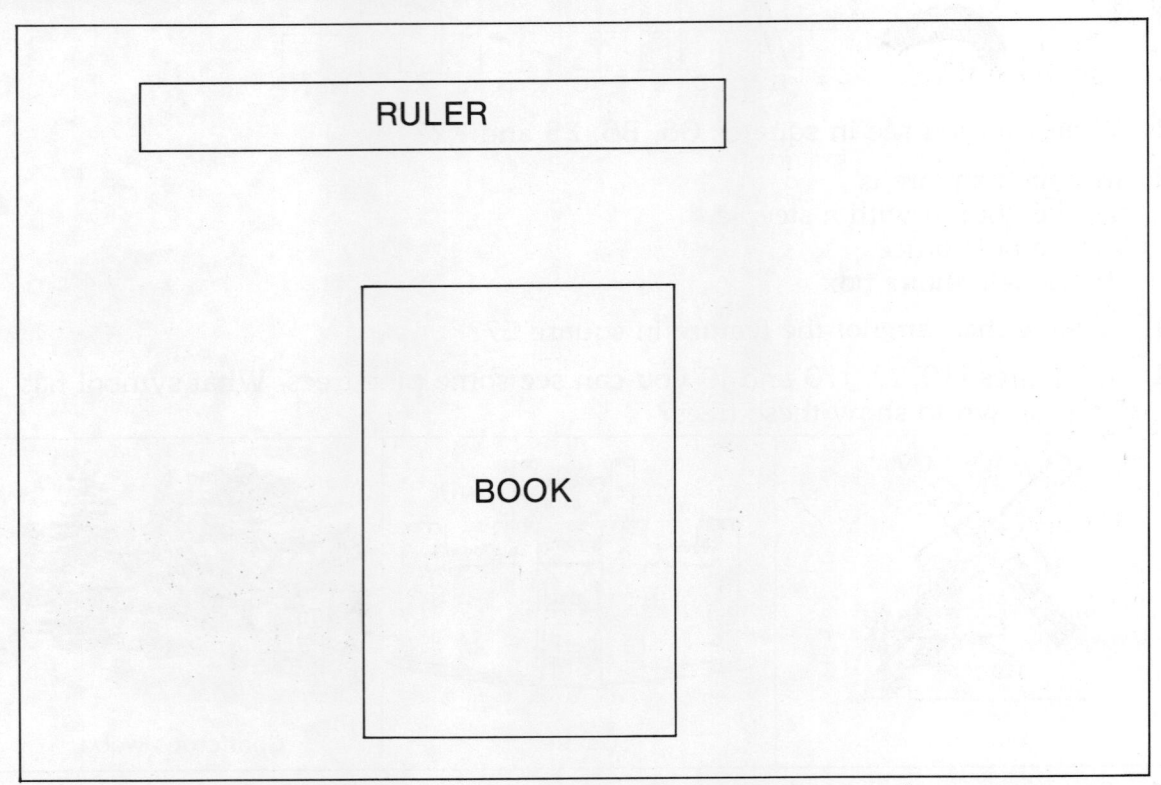

The plan on this page shows a table, drawn to a scale so that every length on the plan is ¼ the real size. This means that the scale of the plan is ¼ or 1:4.

On the plan the table is shown as a rectangle 15cm long. Since this is ¼ the real length, we know the table must be 4 times as big in real life.

What is the real length of the table?

Things to do

Draw a plan of your desk or table to a scale 1/10th of its real size.

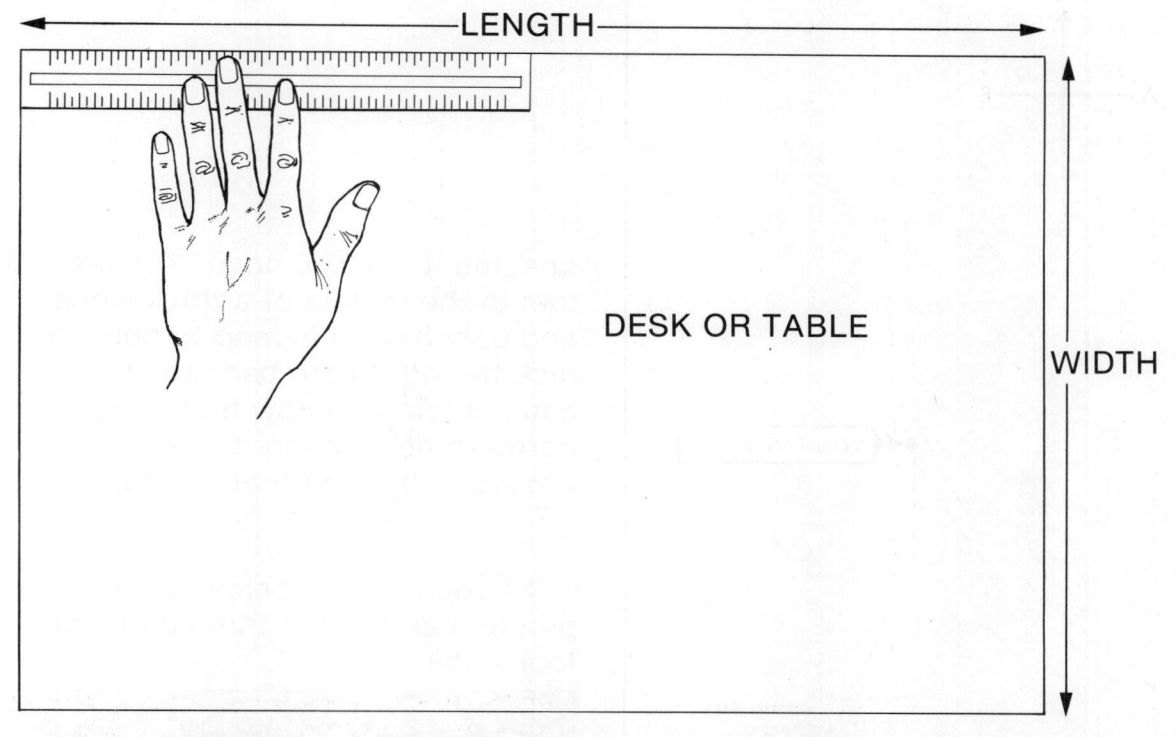

Measure the length of the table in centimetres. Divide by 10. This is the length you will have to measure off on your ruler to show the length of the desk on your plan.

Measure the width of the table from front to back in centimetres. Divide this by 10. This is the width of the table to be shown on your plan.

If the real table is 100cm long and 80cm wide your map will have to measure 10cm by 8cm.

Measure the length of a book and a ruler on your table. Divide these measurements by 10. Draw the book and the ruler on your plan.

If your ruler is 30cm long, what length will it be on your plan?

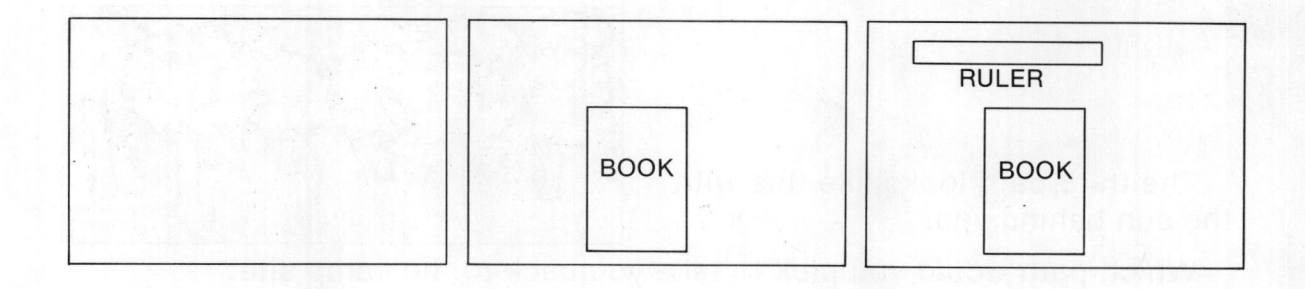

9

Finding your way with a map

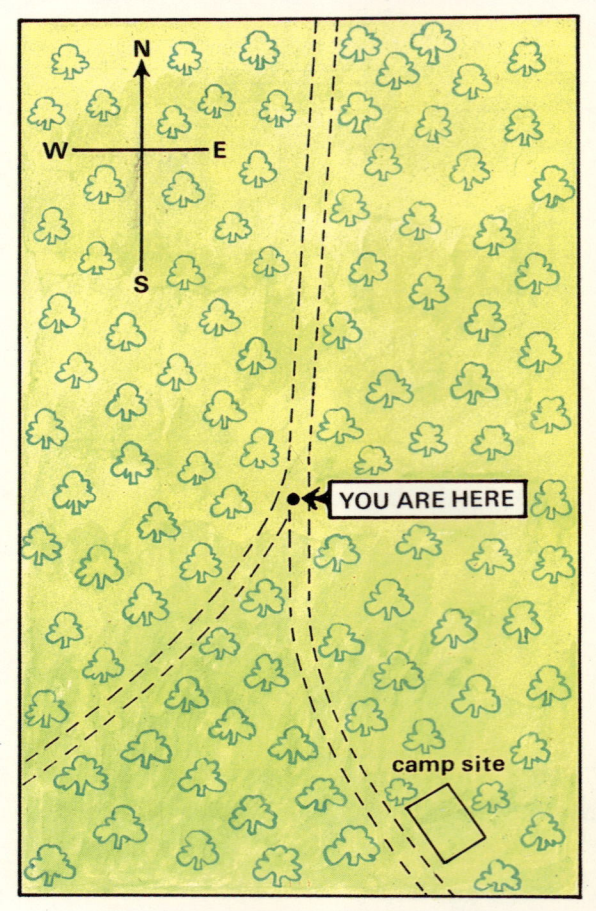

Imagine it is 12.00 noon. You are lost in the middle of a thick wood and only have this map to help you pick the right path back to your camp site. You know that, in the northern hemisphere the sun is always in the south at midday.

As you can see below, your problem is that the three paths all look alike.

The first path looks like this with the sun to your left.

The second path looks like this with the sun straight ahead.

The third path looks like this with the sun behind you.

Which path would you pick to take you back to the camp site?

10

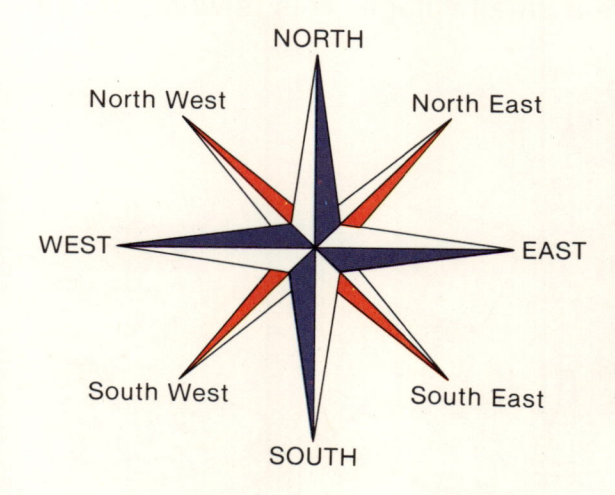

At midday in the northern hemisphere the shadows cast by the sun point north. Knowing where north, east, south and west are can help you to find your way with a map. The directions halfway between north and east, east and south, south and west, and west and north are easy to remember, as you can see from the diagram.

Things to do

Look at this map. Imagine you are standing at the place marked with a large dot. There is a wood to the north of you and an airport to the south.

1. What is the direction from your position to
   1) the church
   2) the windmill
   3) the post office
   4) the telephone box
2. At your school the direction of the sun at midday is south. Work out where north, east and west are as well.
3. Which windows in your school face north? Which face south?

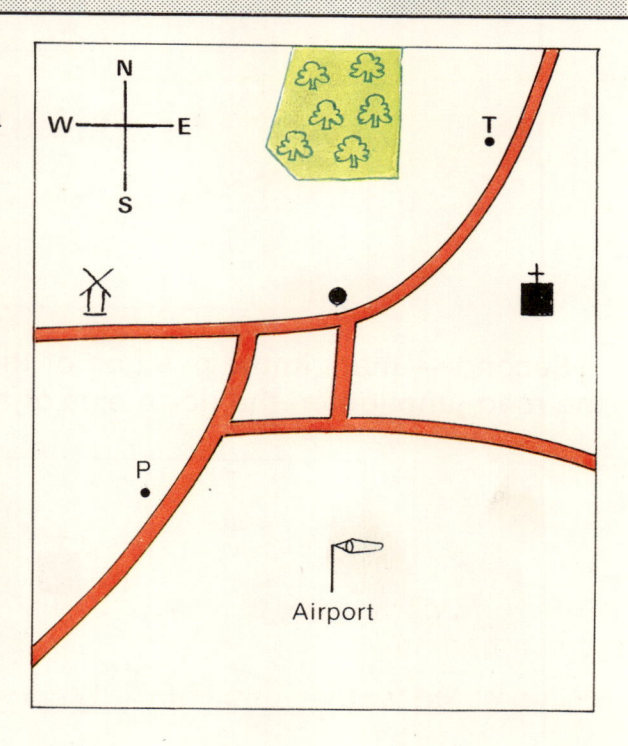

11

Drawing a sketch map

Picture yourself in a helicopter above a small village. This is what you can see from the window looking north.

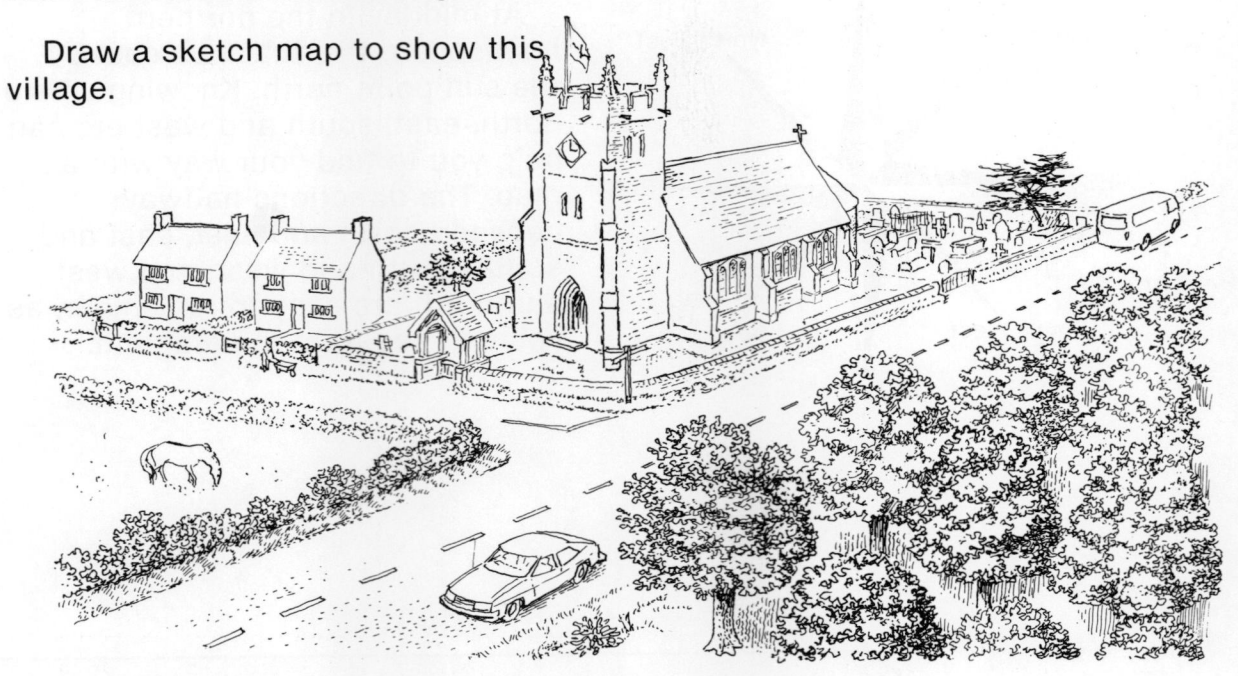

Draw a sketch map to show this village.

First — draw in the main road and the side road.

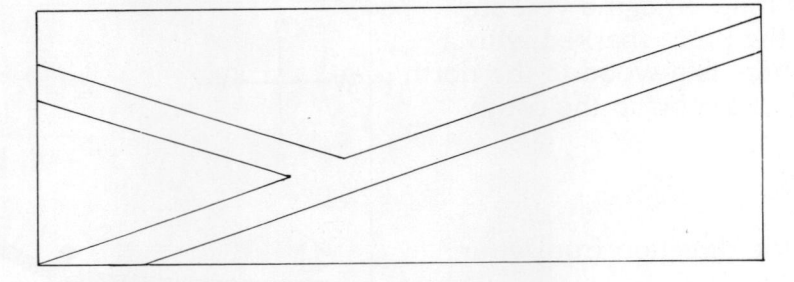

Second — mark in the position of the church. As you can see it is at the road junction on the north side of the road.

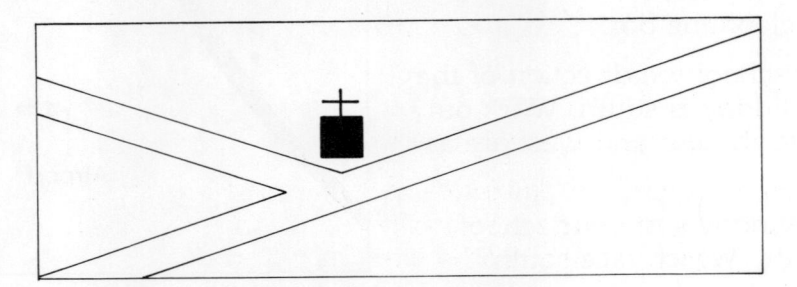

12

Third — draw in the two houses which are on the same side of the road as the church.

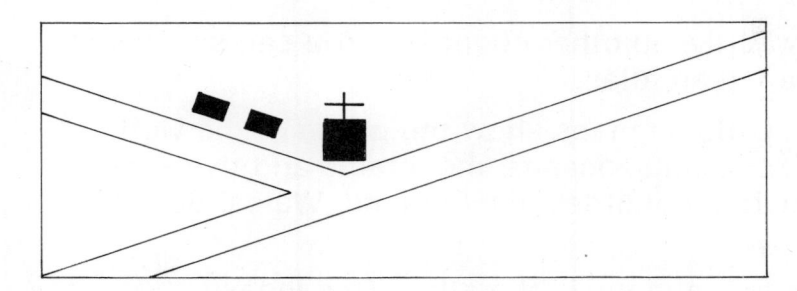

Last — draw small tree symbols to show the wood which is on the south side of the main road.

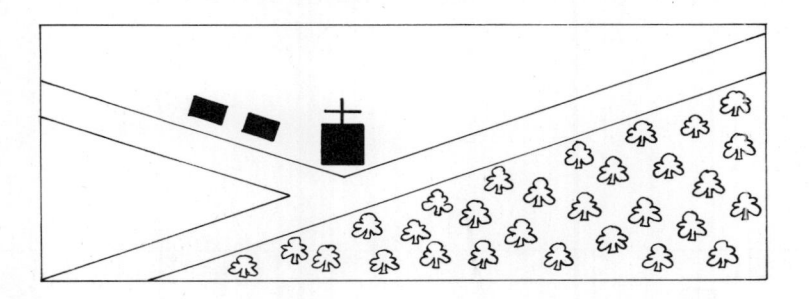

Things to do

1. Draw a sketch map of the village shown in this picture.

2. Draw a sketch map of
   1) your school grounds
   2) your home and the streets nearby

3. Write a description of your journey from home to school. Mention the landmarks you pass. Then try to draw a sketch map to show this journey. Use symbols to show the landmarks you have described.

13

Using an atlas

Some of us have relatives who live in other countries. You can see where they live if you look at a map in an atlas.

An atlas is a book of maps. Some maps show the whole of the world, giving the names of continents, seas, oceans, mountains and rivers. Other maps in the atlas show separate countries like England, Wales, Scotland, France and the United States.

There is usually an index to the maps in the atlas. This index is sometimes called a gazetteer. The placenames are listed in alphabetical order. Against each place there is a page number showing which map to turn to, and also a reference number or letter, like those described on pages 6 and 7.

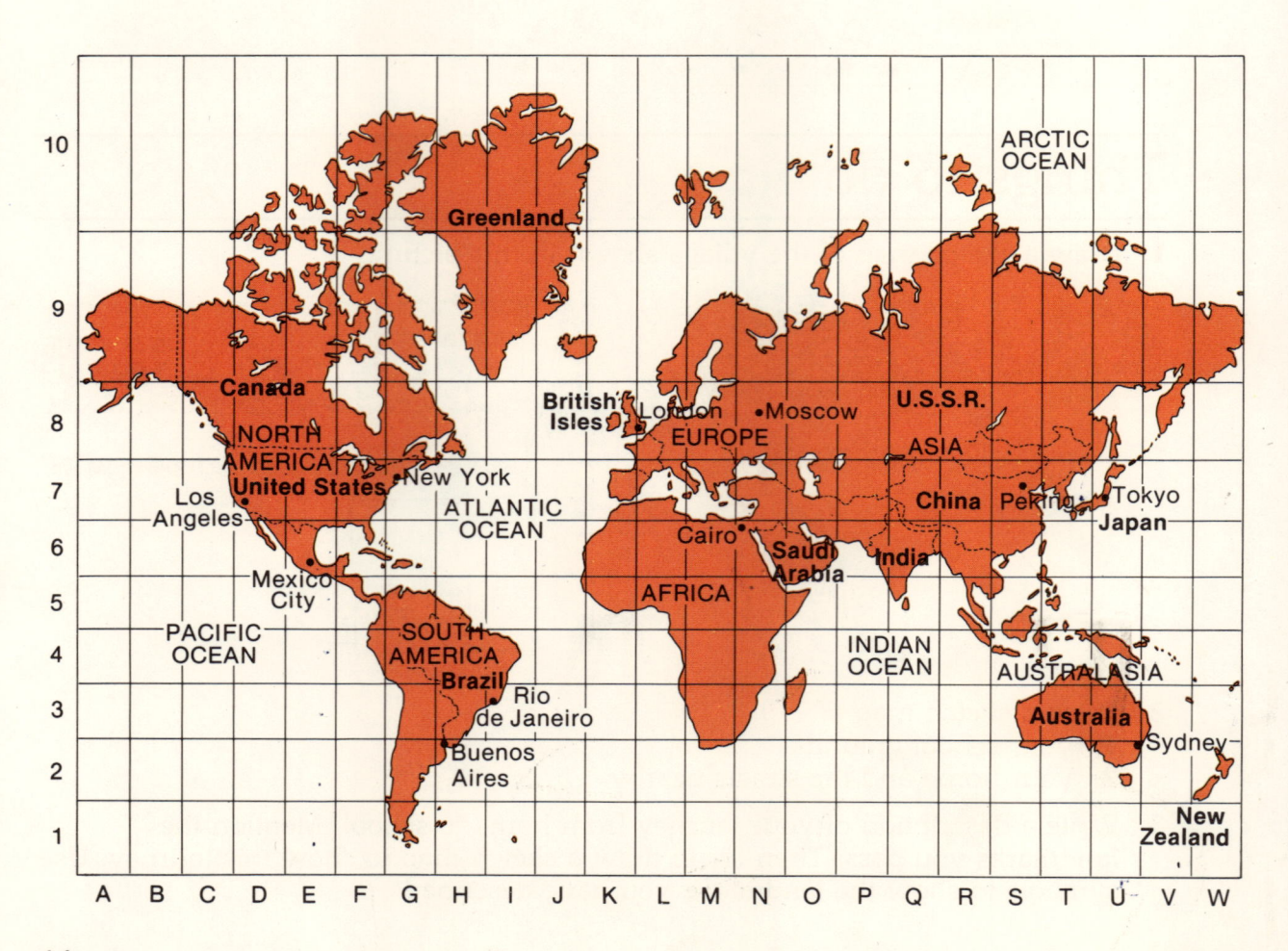

Things to do

The map on the opposite page shows some of the important countries and cities in the world.

1. Look at the map carefully.
   1) Which is the largest continent? Is it Africa, South America, North America, Australasia, Asia or Europe?
   2) Are the British Isles larger or smaller than Canada?
   3) Is Canada larger or smaller than the U.S.S.R.?
   4) Is Moscow east or west of London?
   5) In which direction is New York from London?
   6) Are the British Isles north or south of Africa?
   7) Name two countries which lie to the west of the British Isles.
   8) Which is further from London – Sydney or New York?
   9) What cities are situated in U7, N8, D7, E6?

2. Draw an outline map of the world. Find the names of any towns or countries where you have relatives living abroad. Look these places up in an atlas and then shade or colour them in on your outline map.

Looking at the globe

It used to be hard to believe the earth is round. But no one doubts that now. Cameras on board spaceships have sent back photographs from outer space, showing the earth looking like a football.

Because the earth is completely round, it is not possible to draw a flat map which can show it as it really is. You can test this for yourself if you peel an orange or an apple and then try to make the peel lie down flat.

If there is a globe in your classroom put your finger on the place where you live. You will find it interesting to see which are the shortest distances between your home, and cities in other parts of the world. You can do this by stretching a piece of thread or string tightly between the two places to find out which is the shortest route.

If you spin the globe you will see that it is tilted. It spins round between two points.

The point at the top of the globe, in the north, is called the North Pole. The point at the bottom of the globe, in the south, is called the South Pole. These are the coldest places on the earth.

Exactly halfway between the two Poles you will see a circle right around the globe. This is the Equator. To the north you can see the Tropic of Cancer and to the south the Tropic of Capricorn. The area close to the Equator is called the Equatorial region, and the area between the two Tropics is called 'the Tropics'. This is the hottest place on the earth.

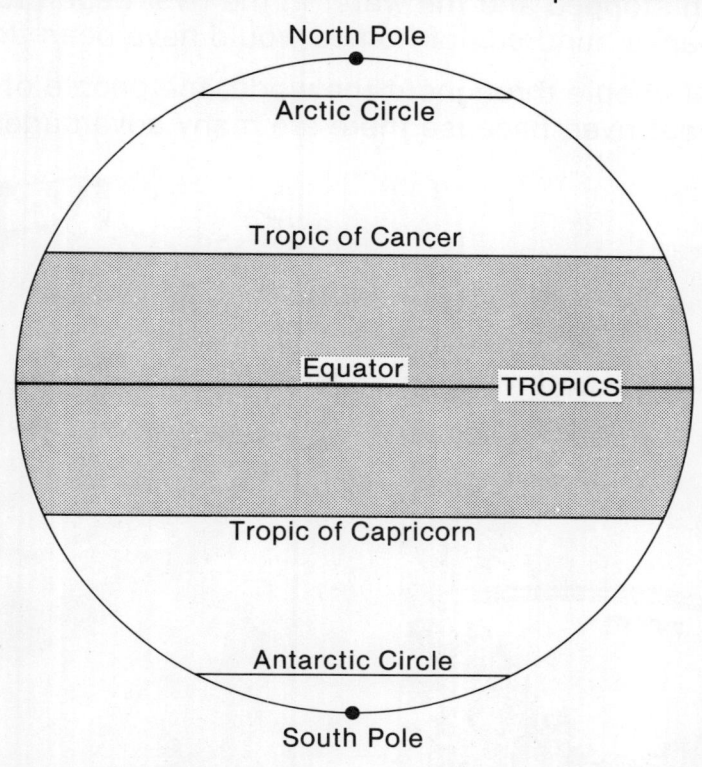

Things to do

1. Look at the world map on page 14. What places would you pass through if you went in a straight line from
   1) London to Tokyo
   2) London to New Zealand
   3) London to New York

2. Now find the shortest route on the globe between these places. What countries would you fly over? Are they the same as those you worked out from the world map? Which routes would you follow if you were a pilot?

3. What advantages has a globe over a world map in an atlas?

Places where people live

Living by a river

The river Thames was very full. After many days of rain the people living in London were afraid the siren might sound at any time to tell them the river Thames was about to flood.

Luckily the rain stopped and the water in the river began to go down. If it had burst its banks hundreds of homes would have been flooded.

Like millions of people throughout the world, the people of London live and work by a great river, because there are many advantages in doing so.

Rivers are very useful. They often provide the water needed in factories and in homes. They are often used by boats and ships to bring food to the town and to take goods made in the town's factories to other places to be sold. Long ago, rivers turned waterwheels which provided power to grind corn, to hammer hot metal into shape, and to sharpen knives and swords.

Rivers are also useful because they often have wide valleys and these are good places to build roads and railways. It is easier to build a road or railway if the land is fairly level and there are no hills in the way.

Living near a big river can have some disadvantages. Bridges and tunnels have to be built so that people can cross over to the other side.

Places close to the river are often damp.

When the level of water in the river gets too high it floods over the banks. Low-lying fields and streets near the river become covered with water. This is why builders usually try to avoid building houses on land which they know is easily flooded. Instead they build on ground which is higher. In the countryside the flat land near a river is often left as grassland for cows and sheep.

The place where a river starts is called its source. The place where it ends is called the mouth of the river.

The source of a river is usually on the side of a hill or mountain. Rain falls on the slopes of the hills and the rainwater trickles into pools and then eventually into small streams which take it to the main river.

The river gets bigger as other streams join it. These are called tributaries.

In the hills and mountains the water in the river is usually clear and fresh. There are often waterfalls, deep pools, large boulders and many stones on the bed of the river. These are moved downstream, together with soil and parts of the river bank, when the river is full after days of heavy rain. In this way the river takes rocks and soil from the hills and carries them downstream to a lake or to the sea.

Lower down the river begins to swing from one side of the valley to the other. These bends are called meanders. The stones in the bed of the river have been worn down now and are only small pebbles. In many places there are banks of mud and sand in the course of the river. The river becomes wide and deep and moves more slowly than it did in the hills.

As the river gets closer to its mouth it moves very slowly indeed. It comes at last to the point where the tide comes up the river twice a day. This part of a river, where the sea comes in, is called the estuary.

A lot of the mud carried by the river falls on the bed of the river here. Sometimes there is so much mud it blocks the river mouth and begins to form small islands. The river splits up into several channels and carries more mud to the sea. The muddy mouth of the river juts out into the sea and forms a delta.

Things to do

1. Copy the picture on these pages and name the different parts of the river — source, waterfall, pool, meander, delta and mouth.

2. Which is the nearest river to your school? Is it a slow or a fast stream? Is it muddy? Write a few words to describe this river.

3. Write a few sentences to say why many towns have been built on the banks of rivers.

4. Find out on which rivers these towns are situated — Glasgow, Liverpool, Paris, Cairo, Montreal, New Orleans, Newcastle, Prague, Shanghai.

Living in the mountains

'Those children should never have been allowed to climb the mountain, dressed only in light clothes and gym shoes. They didn't even have warm jumpers to wear.' The leader of the Mountain Rescue Team was very angry. She had risked her life in a blizzard to rescue a group of children who had been caught out by an unexpected snowstorm.
'They think that because it is warm and sunny when they set off, it will stay like that all day,' she said.

As she well knew, hills and mountains usually get more rain and snow than the valleys below. It is always colder at the top of a mountain than at the bottom. The higher the mountain is, the colder it gets near the top.

In a hot part of Africa there is a very high mountain called Kilimanjaro. Despite the tropical plants and jungle animals at its foot, the top of the mountain, called the summit, is always white with snow.

If you climbed a mountain like Kilimanjaro you would start your journey among tropical plants and trees, and then climb through mountain pastures and pine trees until you reached the ice and thick snow at the summit.

You can see these different parts of a mountain in the picture.

tropical rain forests and savanna

mountain peak

cool mountain pastures

coniferous forests

cooler mountain slopes

In Britain the mountains are not high enough to be covered in snow all the year round. In Switzerland the Alps are over three times as high as any of the mountains in Britain. There the mountain summits are always covered in snow and ice, even in the hottest summers. Rivers of ice, called glaciers, can be seen in some of the high mountain valleys of the Alps.

The Alps were formed about thirty million years ago, when the earth's surface started to crumple up in places. You can picture what happened like this — Take a piece of paper and hold it in both hands. Push your hands together and watch the paper crumple up or fold over to make a series of mountains.

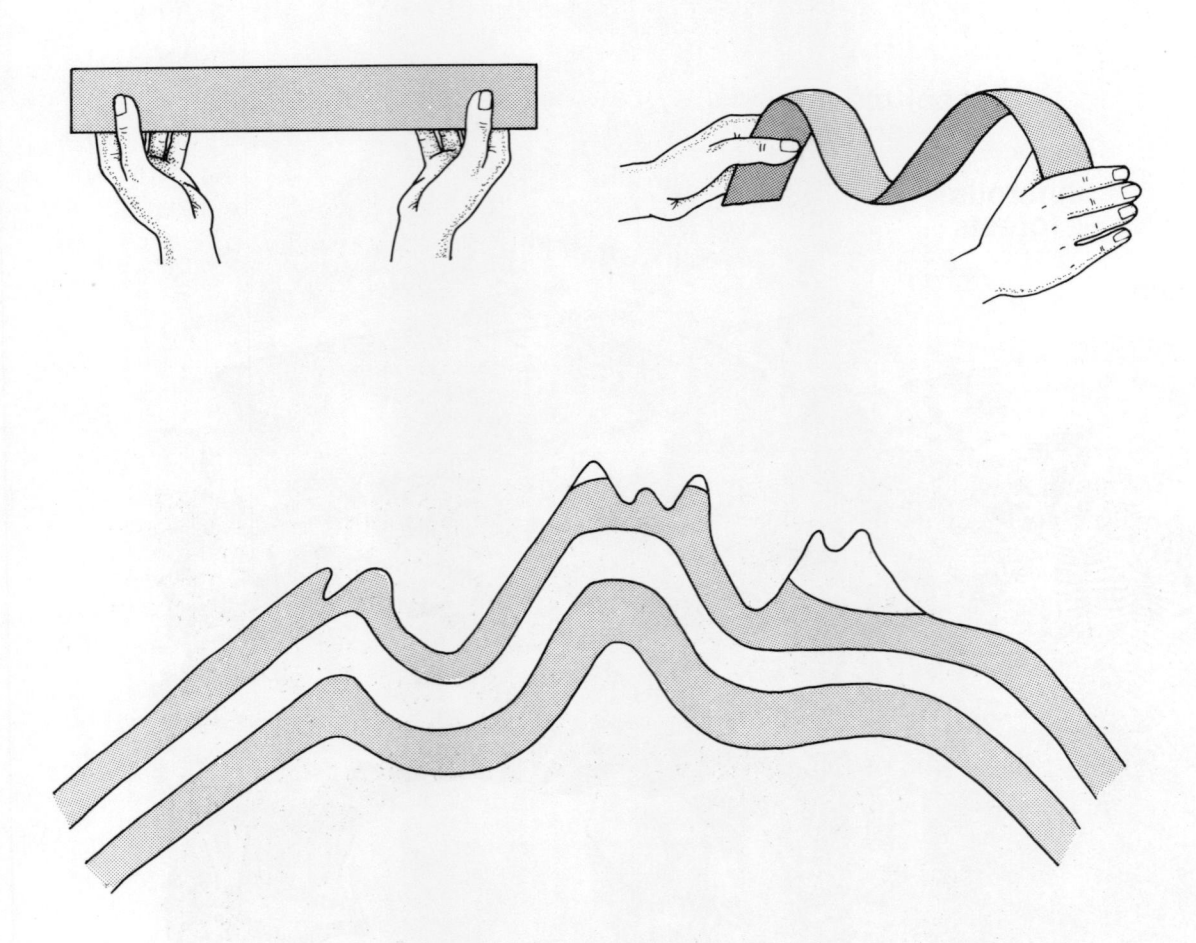

The rocks in the photograph opposite were folded like this.

Many hills and mountains in Britain have flat summits. Highland which is flat-topped is called a plateau. Lowland which is flat is called a plain.

Folded rocks at Lulworth in Dorset

Very few people live in the mountains. Those who do often get work in the forests, planting and cutting trees. Some work on farms and look after flocks of sheep or the cattle which graze on the mountain pastures in summer when the snow has melted on the lower slopes.

Some people earn a living from the people who come to the mountains on holiday. Workers are needed to run the hotels and gift shops, and to work in the places where you can ski in winter.

Things to do

1. If you walked down a mountain path from the summit, would you expect the weather to get warmer or colder near the foot of the mountain? Would you expect to get more or less rain?

2. Draw a picture of a very high mountain in a hot land. Write on your picture the names of the different things you might expect to see if you climbed to the summit.

3. Write a few sentences to say why only a few people live in the mountains.

4. Copy the picture below and name the three features lettered A, B, C.

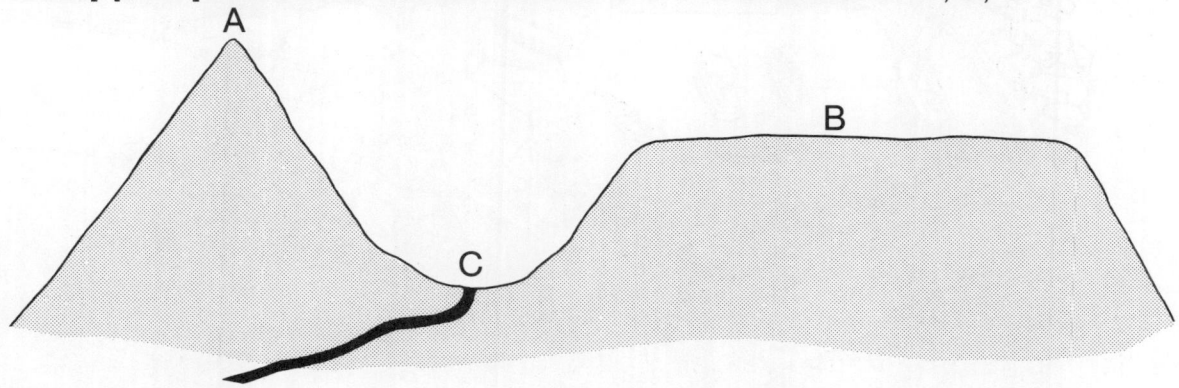

25

Living at the coast

On 1 February 1953, many frightened people had to leave their homes in towns like King's Lynn and Hunstanton, in Eastern England, when the North Sea broke through the sea walls and flooded many seaside homes. Over 300 people were drowned or killed.

The same storms caused great destruction to the low-lying coast of Holland as well. Waves damaged 40,000 houses there and over 1,800 people died. Many fishing ports, harbours and seaside resorts suffered harm.

Rescuing a horse during the Great Flood of 1953

It was a terrible reminder of the power of the sea. This is why you can often see high sea walls and embankments at the seaside. They have been built to hold back the waves in times of storm. Otherwise the sea would destroy the coast.

At Dunwich in Suffolk, a town which was prosperous in medieval times, has been washed away by the sea. In other parts of Britain ports which were once important have had their harbours blocked by sand.

Many of the towns at the coast are ports. They have docks where cranes are used to load containers filled with goods to be sent to other ports around the world. At the same time food and other goods are unloaded from ships from other lands. London, Liverpool, Glasgow, Bristol, Dublin and Southampton are all important ports in Britain. Find these towns on a map.

Some ports are well known for their fishing harbours. These are exciting and colourful places when the fishing boats come in to port. Cod, herring, plaice, lobsters and other fish are unloaded on to the quayside and sold. Grimsby, Hull, Aberdeen, Lowestoft and Fleetwood are important fishing ports in Britain.

Many towns by the coast are important because they are seaside resorts with sandy beaches and attractive cliffs. The most important thing about many of them is that they are near the big cities of Britain where most people live.

This is why Brighton, near London, is a very important seaside resort even though it has a pebble beach. It is easy to get to.

Many coasts in Britain have cliffs like those you can see in these pictures.

headland

waves

Cliffs often jut out into the sea on either side of a bay. Cliffs like this are called headlands.

The cliffs have been cut away by the waves. In a gale the waves thunder against the shore with great force. They crash stones and pebbles from the beach against the cliffs and these dislodge the rocks at the bottom, causing those above to topple over.

If the rocks are worn away on either side of a headland a bit of the cliff may be left behind as an island. This is called a stack.

You can sometimes see a stack still joined by an arch to the headland.

stack

arch

cave

The arch was a cave at first. The waves cut away the rocks and made the cave deeper until at last it was cut through to form an arch.

A sandy beach

A pebble beach

In between the headlands there are bays. These sometimes have pebble beaches. The pebbles are simply rocks from the cliffs which have been cut away by waves and then rounded as they crash against the cliffs and against each other during a storm.

In time the pebbles are ground down into smaller and smaller bits of rock, until there is nothing left but sand.

Things to do

1. Draw a picture of a headland and show on your picture a stack, an arch, a cave and a pebble beach.
2. Write two or three sentences to say what can happen when there is a storm at sea and giant waves crash against the shore.
3. What are these towns noted for
   Bristol, Fleetwood, Brighton, Southampton, Grimsby?
4. Describe a seaside resort you have been to on holiday, or for a day visit. Draw a picture to show one of the interesting things you saw at the coast there.

Living in a desert

It is the middle of the day in a town in the desert. The heat is so great and the sun so bright that most of the townspeople are indoors or sitting in the shade of a tree or in the shadow of a building.

If you visited the desert at this time you would probably wear a big hat with a wide brim to keep your head in the shade. Or you might prefer to wear Arab clothes like those you can see in the picture. These people are wearing the burnous.

This is the name given to the long, loose-fitting gown which many Arabs wear. As you can see it reaches right down to the ground. It is very cool to wear because it shades the body from the sun. The burnous is often white in colour because white doesn't heat up as quickly as dark colours like black. The hood keeps the head cool and stops sand getting in the eyes.

The modern homes in this desert town have only a few windows with shutters to keep out the sun and verandahs to make a shady place to keep cool outside in the heat. In the old mud houses which can still be seen in the desert lands, there are narrow slits in the thick walls instead of windows. Large glass windows, like those in modern homes in Britain, would heat up like a greenhouse in a desert town. This isn't a problem for wealthy Arabs since the homes of rich people can be made cool with the aid of air-conditioning machines.

Many Arabs are rich because oil has been discovered in the desert lands — far more than is needed by the people for their own use. They sell it abroad and some of the money which they get for their oil is spent on hospitals, television stations, modern roads and luxury motor cars. Yet many Arabs are still poor. The deserts are a mixture of old and new.

Only a few Arabs, called the Bedouin, still travel by camel across the deserts, and live in tents. Camels are useful animals to have with you in the desert since they feed on desert plants, and go for days without water or food, have feet which grip the desert sands and stones and eyelashes which keep out the flying sand.

We often think of the deserts as places where there is sand everywhere. In fact most deserts are rocky or pebbly rather than sandy. Hills and mountains stand out like those seen in the picture. You have probably seen views like this in cowboy films. The mountains have rocky summits and have been carved into fantastic shapes. At the foot of a desert mountain there are usually great heaps of stones.

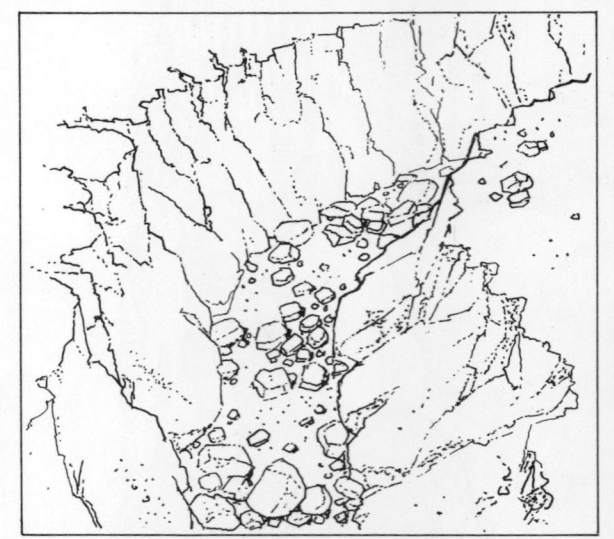

The desert valleys, called wadis, only have rivers or streams in them when it rains. Because there is so little rain in the desert lands travellers sometimes camp in a wadi for a night's sleep. This is a dangerous thing to do. When it rains the wadis fill up very quickly with water and people have been drowned in the middle of a desert.

For most of the year the desert lands are very hot indeed and very dry. This means that only special plants can grow there. Some plants, like the cactus, are called succulents and keep water in their leaves or stems. This water keeps them alive during the long dry periods.

Fresh water is found in only a few places in the deserts — usually at a well or sometimes as a spring. These places with water are called oases.

At an oasis the water helps plants to grow such as the date palm. These date palms are a very welcome sight for travellers in the desert, whether they are driving motor vehicles or riding on camels.

Things to do

1. Imagine you have been on an expedition into the centre of the Sahara Desert. Picture what would happen if your car ran out of petrol and you discovered that there were no spare cans of petrol left. Write a story describing your adventures and saying how you eventually managed to find your way to the oasis seen in the picture on this page.
2. Why are camels useful animals in the desert?
3. Write down five things about the Arab way of life which tell you that they live in a place where the weather is hot and dry.

When a volcano erupts

Just before lunch on a hot day in August in the year 79 A.D. the people of Pompeii were horrified to see a huge cloud of smoke and ash rising above the volcano Vesuvius, a few kilometres from their town.

Minutes later hot ash and scorching cinders started to fall on Pompeii itself. Stifling hot gases caused many people to suffocate. A baker ran away from his shop in such a panic he left the day's takings behind. We know this because the ash and cinders covering Pompeii helped to keep the contents of the houses in a good state of preservation until they were discovered many hundreds of years later.

Vesuvius erupted because deep below the earth's surface the rocks are very hot indeed. A weak point in the surface allowed this hot rock to pour out as lava. Lava is liquid or molten rock.

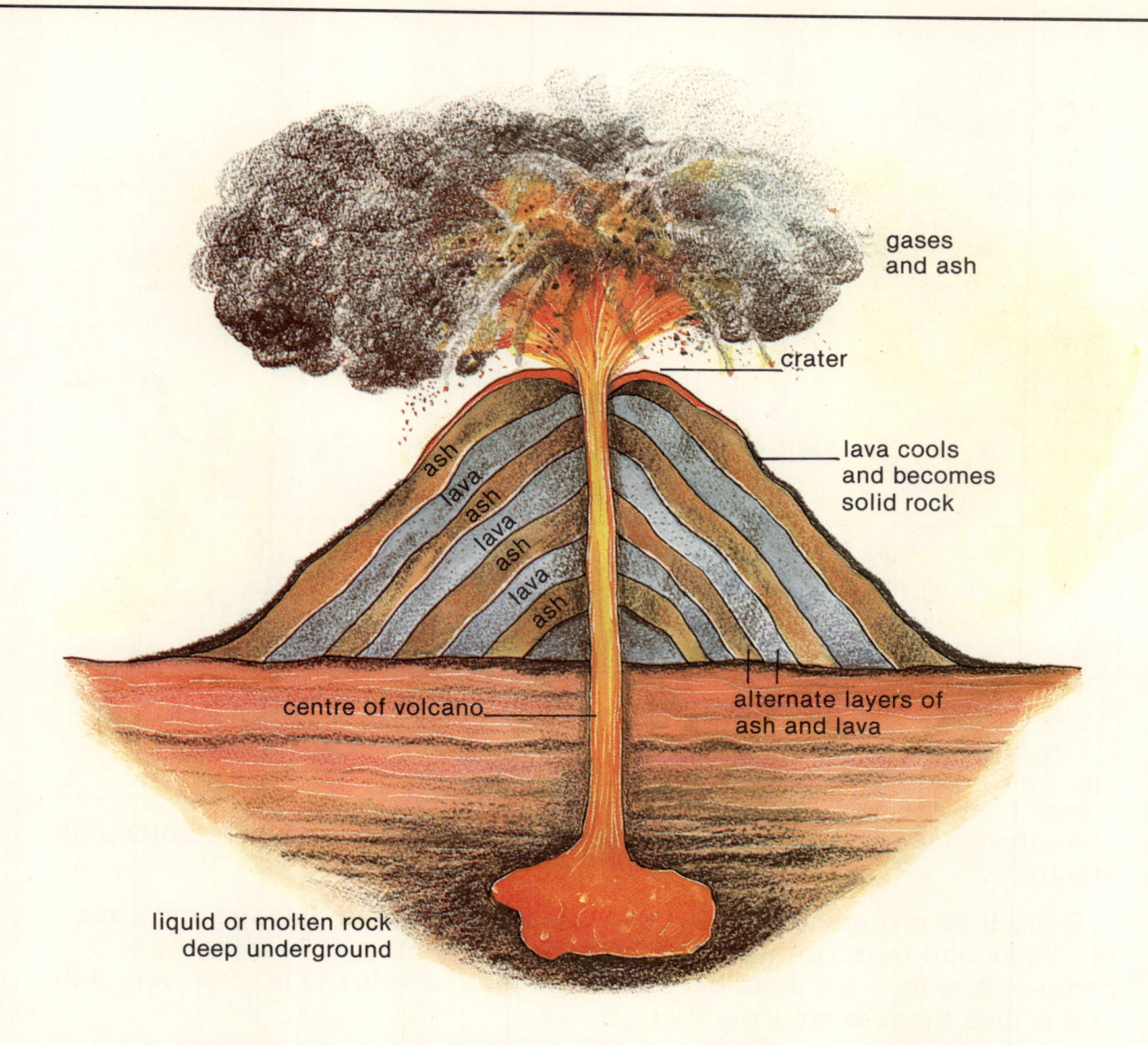

Diagram labels:
- gases and ash
- crater
- lava cools and becomes solid rock
- ash, lava, ash, lava, ash, lava, ash, lava, ash
- centre of volcano
- alternate layers of ash and lava
- liquid or molten rock deep underground

Volcanoes can be seen erupting in many parts of the world today. Sometimes the lava comes fast, forcing up the rocks above and causing the volcano to explode with a bang showering hot ash and cinders into the air. The blast makes a deep hole in the summit of the volcano. This is called a crater.

Afterwards molten lava flows down the sides of the volcano, covering the ash. When it cools it forms a hard layer of rock over the layer of ash underneath. In this way a volcano grows, layer by layer, until it becomes a high mountain.

Not all volcanoes erupt so violently. Some are active all the time but the lava just bubbles quietly in the crater and scientists can get near enough to take photographs. Volcanoes which erupt regularly are called active volcanoes. Those which have not erupted for many thousands of years and thought to be dead, are called extinct volcanoes. Those which erupt very occasionally with long intervals in between are called dormant volcanoes.

KEY
earthquakes
volcanoes

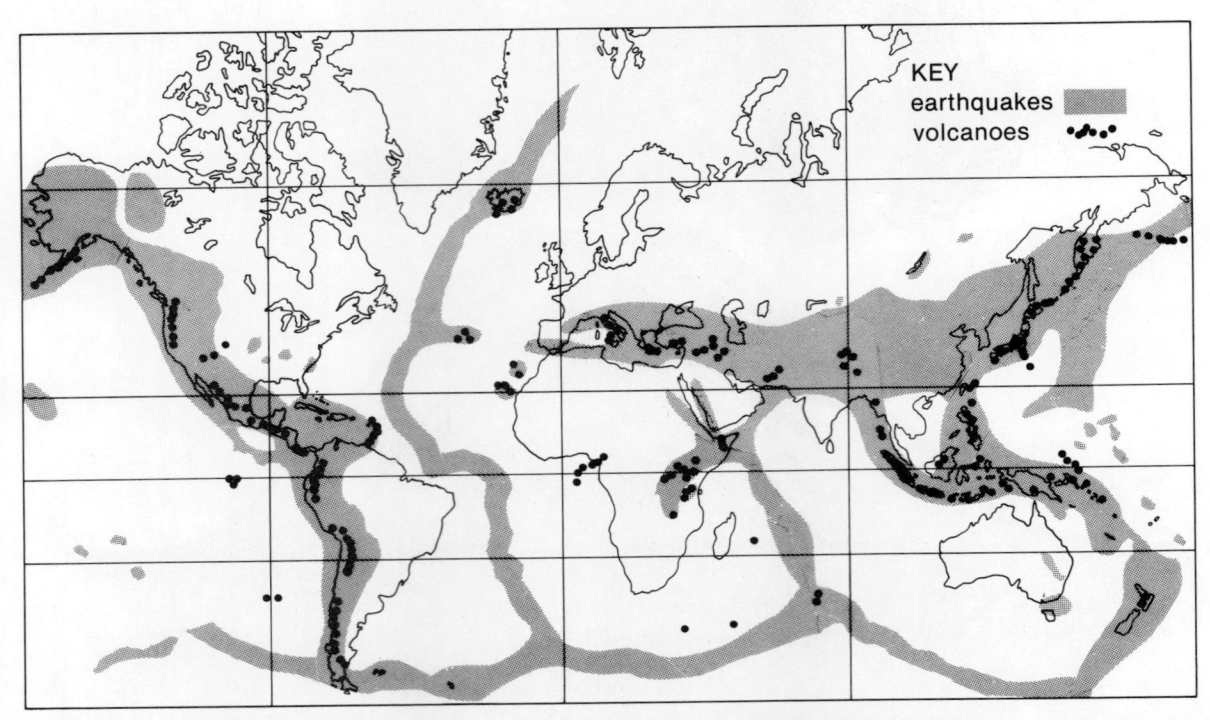

All the volcanoes in Britain are extinct, like the volcano where Edinburgh stands.

Every time a volcano erupts it can cause widespread damage and cover the fields and farms on its slopes with ash or even lava. Despite the danger, farmers work there because the soil on a volcano is often very rich and allows them to grow good crops.

The areas of the world where there are many earthquakes also happen to be the areas where many volcanoes are to be found. This is because volcanoes are often formed where there is a crack in the earth's surface.

Things to do

1. Copy the map using coloured dots for the volcanoes and a light colour for the area where earthquakes are likely to happen.

2. Which of these areas are well away from earthquakes and volcanoes?
   England   Iceland   South Africa   China   Iran   Japan

3. Write a few sentences to say how a volcano is formed. Why do farmers sometimes live on the slopes of volcanoes despite the risk of eruption?

4. Make a model of a volcano.

Trace or copy the diagram. Colour it to show the layers of ash and lava. This is called a cross-section and it shows the volcano cut in half. Colour the rest of the volcano to show the fields and farms on the slopes. You can also see the gullies and channels which have been washed away by streams formed by the rain.

Use a pair of scissors to cut out the volcano. Cut carefully along the solid black lines, including those round the top of the crater.

Fold along the dotted lines and paste the glued panel underneath the cross-section panel to complete the model.

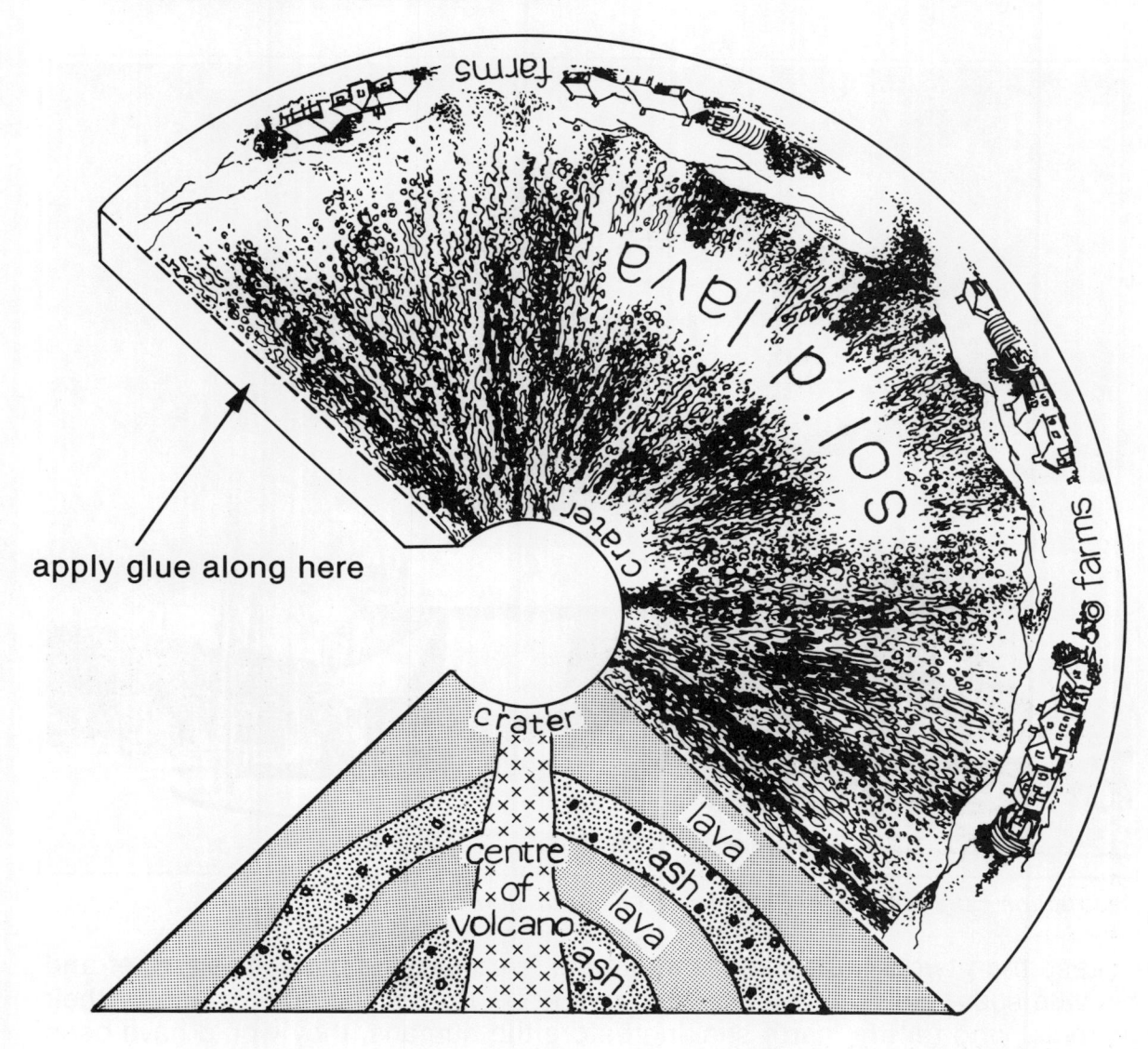

37

Living through an earthquake

Sunday evening, 23 November 1980. Near a small town in Italy a farmer and his wife are startled when their farm animals begin to bellow and scream with fright. Hurriedly leaving their house to see what is wrong, they soon discover the reason. The earth begins to shake and heave.

With a terrifying roar the farm buildings crash to the ground. The farmer and his wife try to run but are thrown to the ground. Great holes open up in front of them.

Destruction caused by an earthquake at Agadir in Morocco

Less than two minutes later the ground is quiet once more. The farmer and his wife soon realise how lucky they have been. But for the noise made by their animals, who felt the earth shaking before the humans, they would have been killed by falling bricks and stones.

They lived through a severe earthquake which killed hundreds of people and destroyed almost all the buildings in a number of small towns in southern Italy.

buckled railway line

burst dam

When an earthquake strikes it is usually along a crack in the earth's surface. Sometimes the ground drops down on one side of this crack, and sometimes the ground is just torn apart. Straight roads bend from side to side after an earthquake, and the surface is buckled up and crumpled.

If a dam bursts thousands may be drowned. In large cities fires may break out and destroy buildings which survived the actual earthquake. This was the main reason why much of San Francisco was destroyed after the earthquake in 1906.

Earthquakes occur in certain areas of the world — often in the places where there are many volcanoes. There is no warning of their coming, so the only thing that can be done is to try to erect buildings which will withstand the shock of an earthquake.

rubble in a street

fire

Things to do

1. When and where did the world's last serious earthquake occur?
2. Draw a picture and write a few words to describe what happens when there is an earthquake.

Rocks and soils

About rocks

The earth's surface is made of rock. As you have seen some rocks are formed when volcanoes erupt and molten lava from deep below the ground cools to form new rocks.

Other rocks are made when rivers and streams bring sand and mud to the sea. The sand and mud drop gently to the bottom and each day extra layers of sand and mud are formed. After millions of years the layers of sand are pressed down so much they cling together to make a rock called sandstone. The mud also clings together to make clay. Other rocks, called limestones, are made from the shells of sea creatures.

Large rounded rocks lying on a beach

We don't often see bare rock on the ground because it is usually covered over with soil and plants or streets and buildings. The best place to look is at the seaside where waves crash against the bare rock of a cliff. You can also see bare rocks at the sides of a river valley or in a stone quarry.

In a town you can sometimes see rock exposed at the bottom of a trench or hole dug by workmen laying a pipeline or looking at cables underground.

Stones in the soil

Pieces of rock can be found easily enough in a handful of soil taken from a patch of waste land, a pebble on a beach, or a stone from the bed of a river.

Things to do

1. Look at a pebble or stone or piece of rock. If possible, use a magnifying glass so that you can examine it in detail.

   1) Find out what the rock is made of. – Is the rock heavy or light, hard or soft, is it rough or smooth to touch?

   2) What colours can you see in the rock? Some rocks are made from a number of small crystals and from other small pieces of rock. Some are shiny, some are dark, some brightly-coloured, and some just black or white.

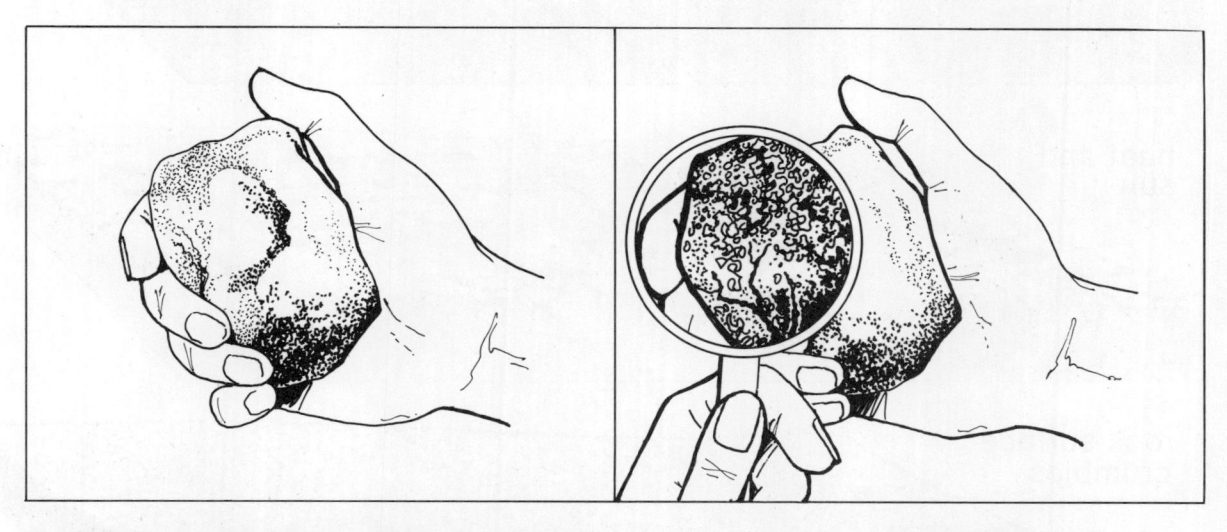

2. When you have finished, write a few words to describe the pebble, stone or piece of rock you have been looking at.

3. Find the names of some different types of rocks.

About soils

Farmers and gardeners need soil in which to grow plants. Some soils feel rough to touch and have tiny pebbles and bits of sand in them. Other soils are soft and smooth, whilst others are very sticky and roll up easily into a mud ball.

This is because the soils come from different types of rock.

Rain falls and gets into the cracks in the rocks. When it is bitterly cold the rainwater in the cracks turns to ice and this causes small pieces of rock to snap off. When it is very hot the heat helps to make the rock on the surface crumble.

Gradually the rocks at the surface split up into hundreds of smaller pieces of rock. Insects find a place to live among these bits of rock. Plants grow too, and their roots help to break down the rocks into smaller pieces. The old roots are left behind when the plants die. Leaves fall from plants and trees and these rot and become part of the soil. Worms burrow among the pieces and turn the soil over.

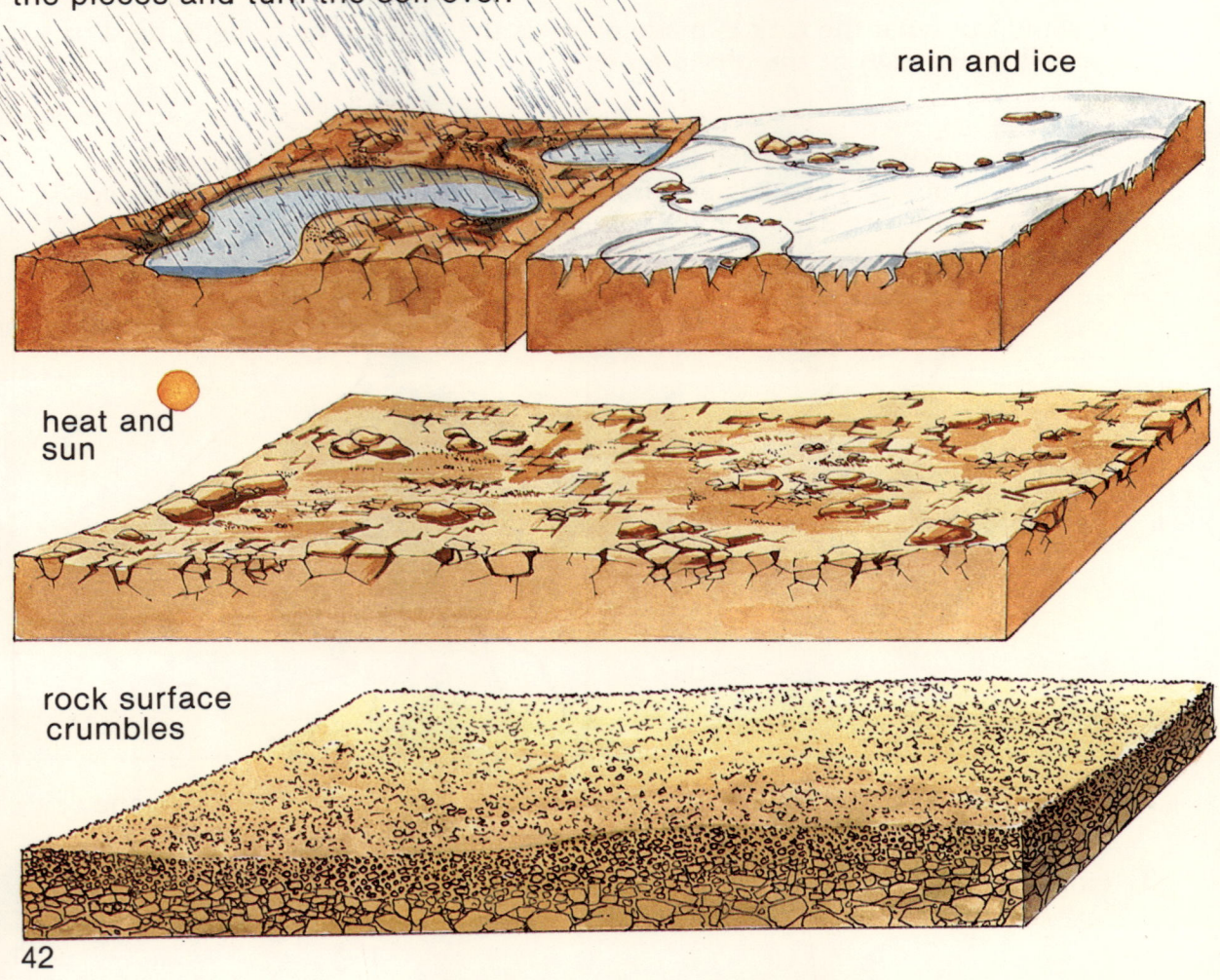

rain and ice

heat and sun

rock surface crumbles

Plants and trees help to make the soil; in turn the soil helps plants and trees to grow. Their roots take water and food from the soil. When the plants die their stalks and leaves rot and help to put back into the soil all the good things which were taken out when the plant was growing.

Things to do

1. You can see something of this if you look carefully at a handful of soil taken from a garden or patch of waste land. Look at the soil carefully through a magnifying glass.
   1) What colour is your soil?
   2) What is the soil made of – can you see any small stones, old leaves, stalks, twigs, or other bits from a tree or plant?
   3) Are there any creatures, such as a worm or insect, in the soil?

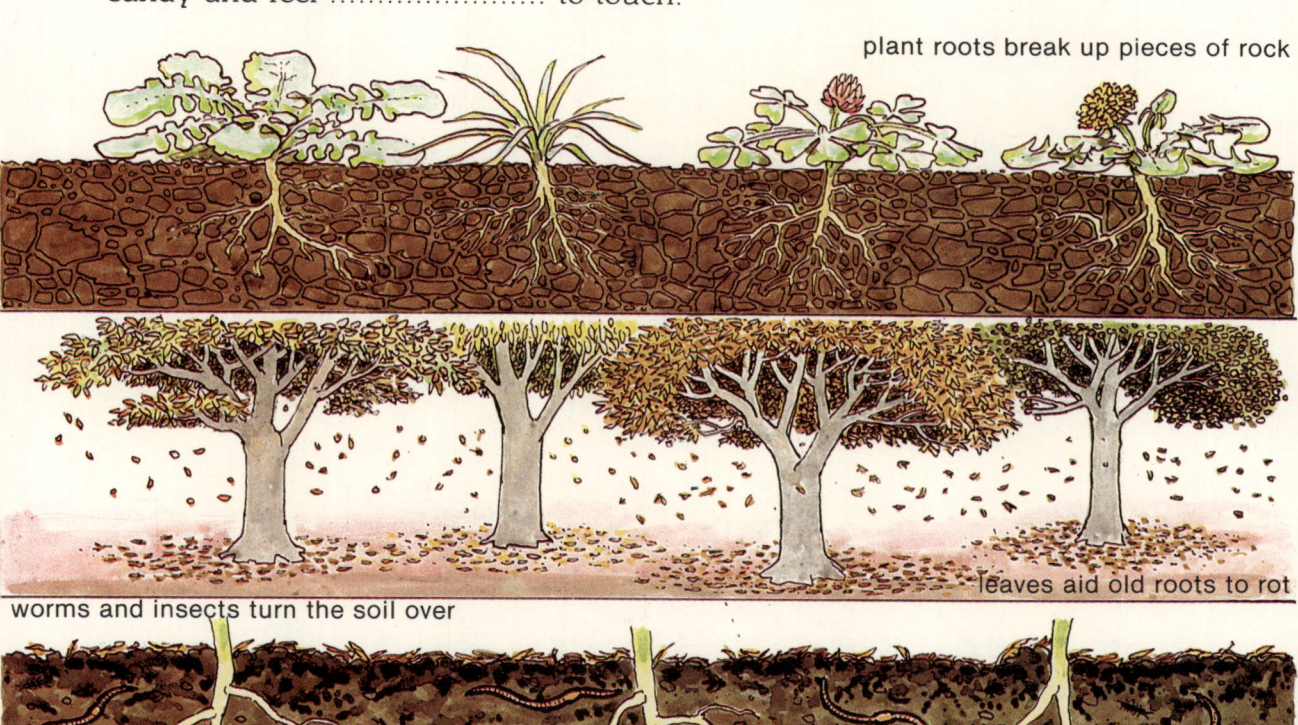

2. Fill in the blanks in these sentences to say what you have found out about soil. Soil is formed from .... The rocks are broken up by the action of the weather and also by .... and .... When plants die .... Some soils are very sticky and .... Others are sandy and feel .... to touch.

plant roots break up pieces of rock

leaves aid old roots to rot

worms and insects turn the soil over

When soil blows away

About fifty years ago a visitor nearing a prairie farm could only just make out the shape of the farm buildings ahead. Even though it was mid-day in July, great clouds of dust filled the air. As the dust settled on the ground, the traveller realised to his horror that it was soil.

For months the weather had been hot and dry. The newly ploughed soil had baked hard and fine dust lay on the surface. Then a gale blew up and soil was rapidly stripped from the land, even though it had taken hundreds of years to form.

Some weeks later there was heavy rain. The floodwaters ripped away the baked dry soil on the slopes of a valley and took it downstream to the sea.

This is called soil erosion. It happens if farmers make it easy for the wind to blow the soil away, or for streams to wash it downwards to the sea. Soil erosion can only be stopped if farmers change their way of farming.

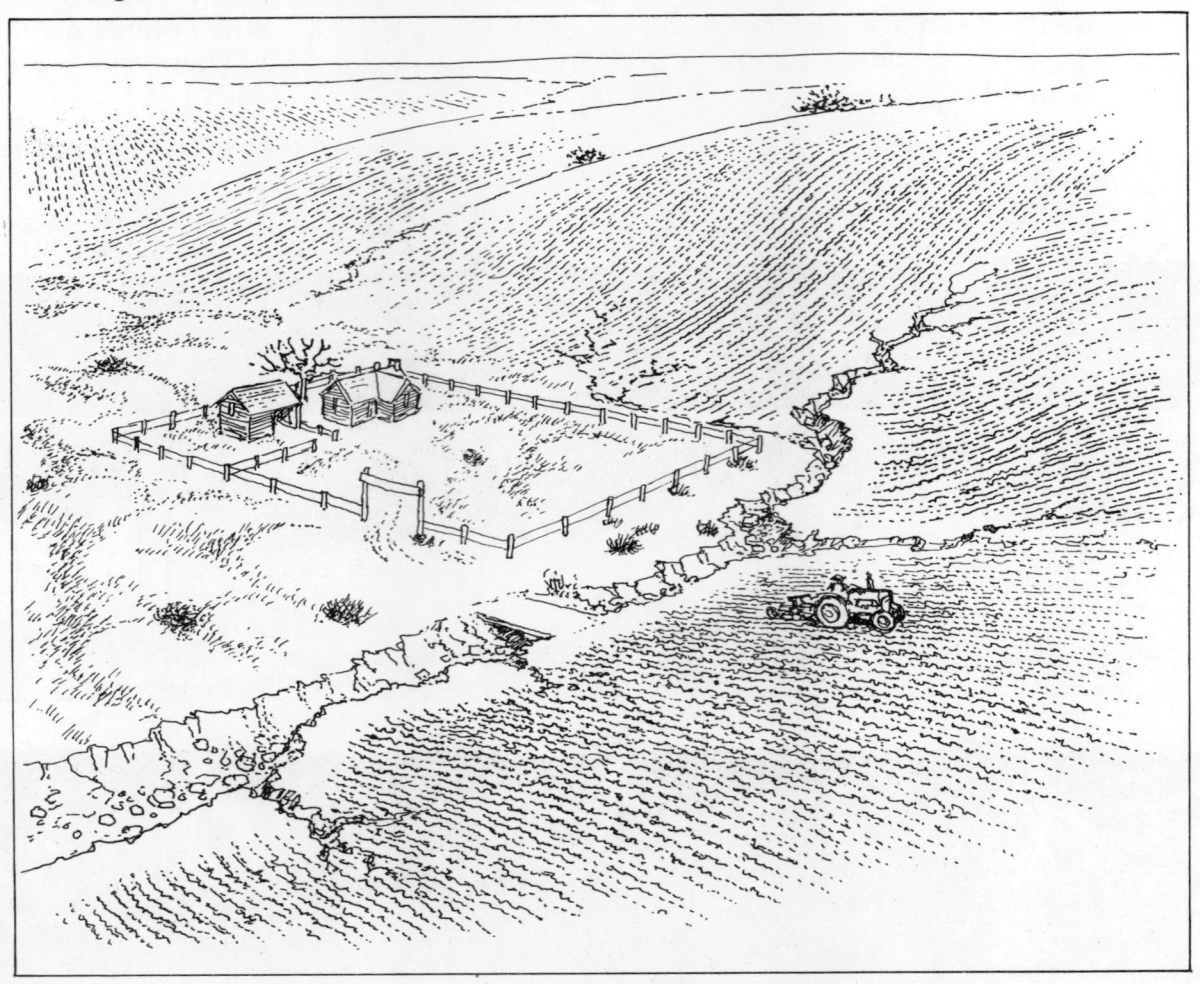

The soil easily blows away if it is dry and dusty, and if there are no trees and plants growing in it with roots to hold the soil together. It is worse if the fields are very large and there are no hedges or walls or clumps of trees to make a windbreak.

Farmers know from past experience that it is often better to keep the old hedges and walls because they lessen the force of the wind.

In dry lands they know that it helps if they can keep the soil well-supplied with water. Moist soil will not blow away.

Things to do

Look at the two pictures. One shows a farm where soil erosion is a problem. The other shows a similar farm but farmed in such a way as to make soil erosion less likely.

1. Copy these pictures and write down the differences you see between them.
2. Write a few words to explain what is meant by soil erosion.

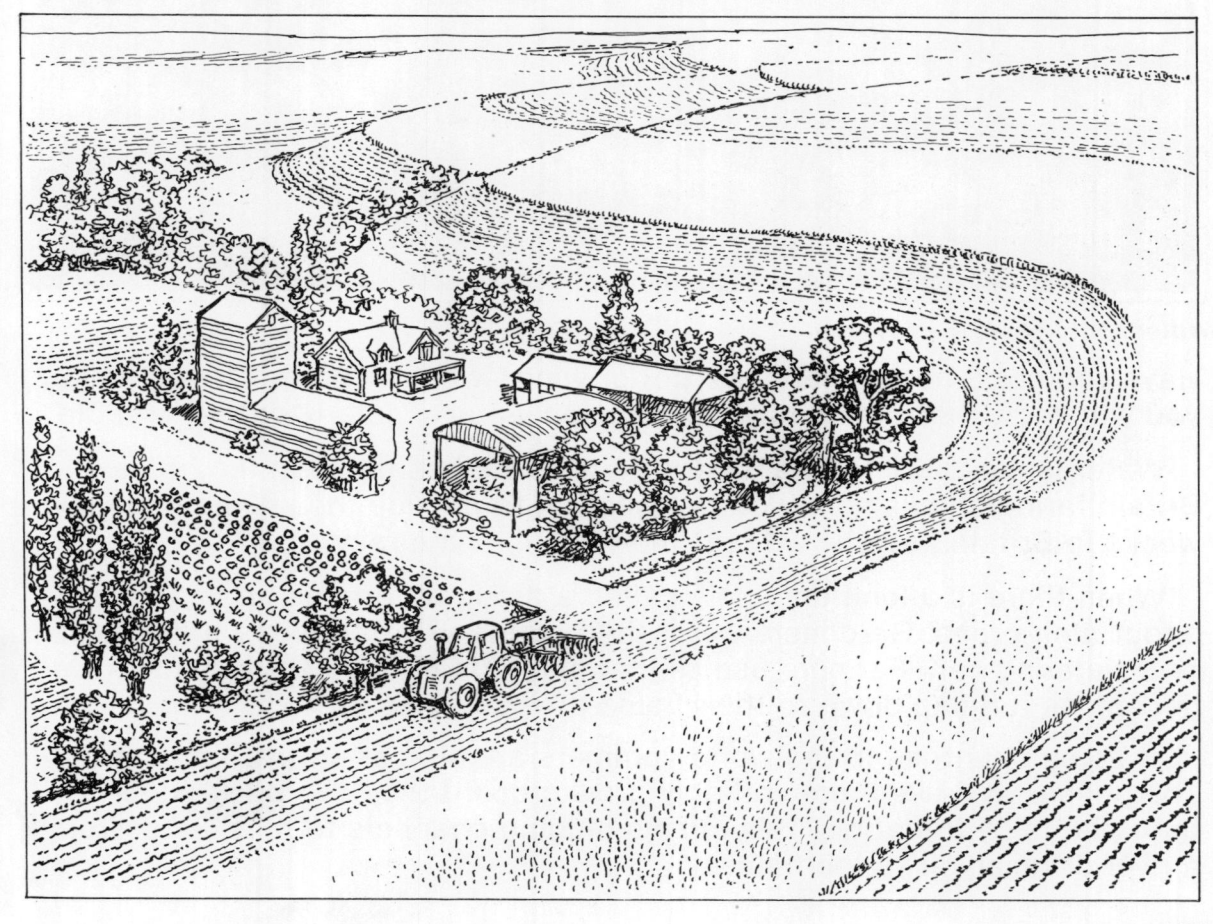

Water

Storing water

Watering a field in East Anglia

Have you got a house plant in a pot or window box at home? If you have you will know that plants have to be given water regularly or they will die.

Water is essential for plants outdoors as well as those in the home. In Britain farmers usually rely on the weather to provide the water, since few weeks in Britain pass by without there being some rainfall.

When there is a long dry spell, called a drought, farmers begin to worry about their crops. Gardeners water their plants with the aid of a hosepipe or a watering can. Farmers use similar methods if they can — some have hosepipes running down to their fields of vegetables or fruit.

In some countries in the world summers are almost always hot and dry. The people who live there can only grow crops if they can bring water to their plants by irrigation. This means digging channels to take water from a river or reservoir to the fields.

dam

irrigation channels

You would see a number of different methods of irrigation if you went to Egypt to the valley of the river Nile. Some Egyptian farmers still use irrigation methods which might have been seen at the time of the Pharaohs. Even then, 5,000 years ago, there was a mud dam across the Nile.

waterwheel

shaduf

Some water is taken from the river in buckets with the aid of a shaduf. This is a pole with a bucket at one end and a heavy weight on the other, so that it can be swung round easily. The bucket is dipped into the river and fills with water. It is then swung round and emptied into a long irrigation channel.

Water is sometimes taken from the river in buckets attached to waterwheels.

47

Much of the water used for irrigation in Egypt is taken from Lake Nasser. This artificial lake was formed when the Aswan High Dam was built across the Nile in 1970. The dam, which is over 100 metres high, feeds water into the irrigation channels which take it to the fields.

This is how engineers build a dam across a great river.

First they choose a place where the valley is narrow and where the valley sides are high so that the water in the reservoir will be deep.

Then they build a smaller dam, called a coffer dam, to keep the river away from the place where the main dam will be built. Sometimes the river is taken through tunnels to divert its course.

Then the main dam is built with a huge sloping pile of earth, stones and clay which will stop the water finding a way through.

The steep concrete wall on the side away from the lake is all that can be seen of the huge dam when it is complete. The tunnel is closed and the river level rises behind the dam to form a huge and deep lake.

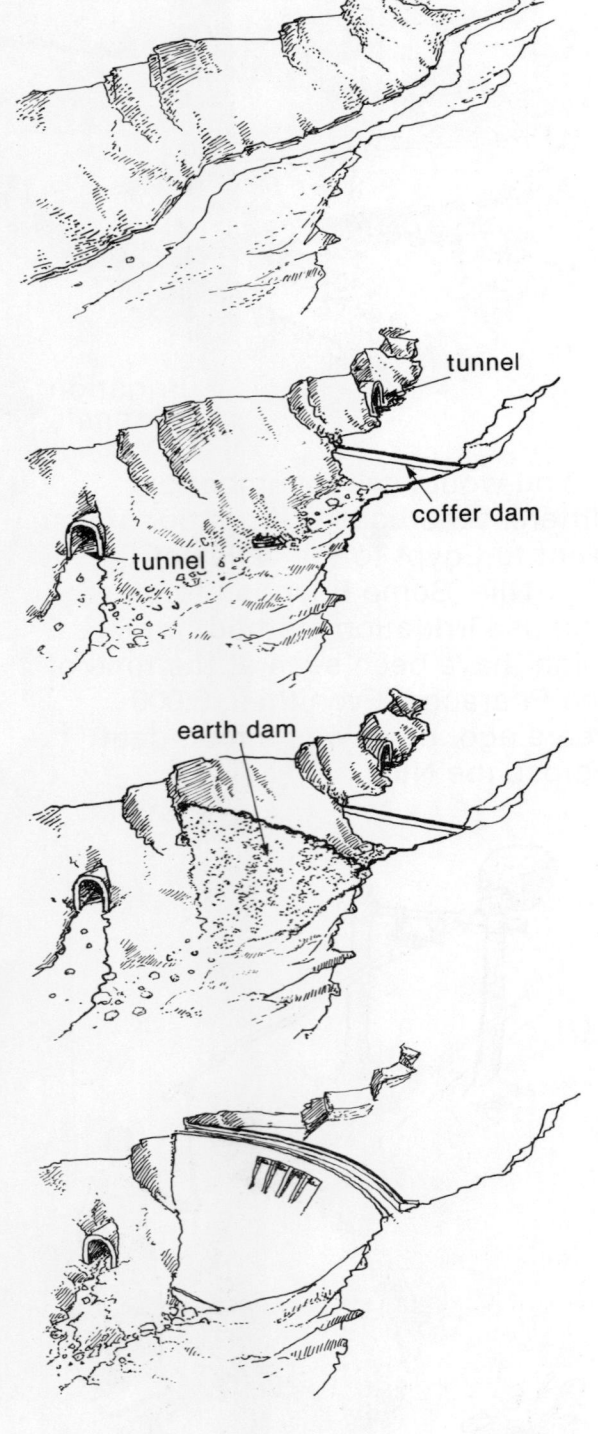

In Britain many dams have been built to store water but not for irrigation. The water is used to supply the great cities with the water they need for use in homes and in factories.

Some dams are used to make hydro-electricity. Water from the dam flows through tubes at high speed and turns the engines which make electricity.

Reservoirs are also useful as places for yachting and fishing, and sometimes for boats and ships taking passengers or goods to places at the other side of the lake or further up the river.

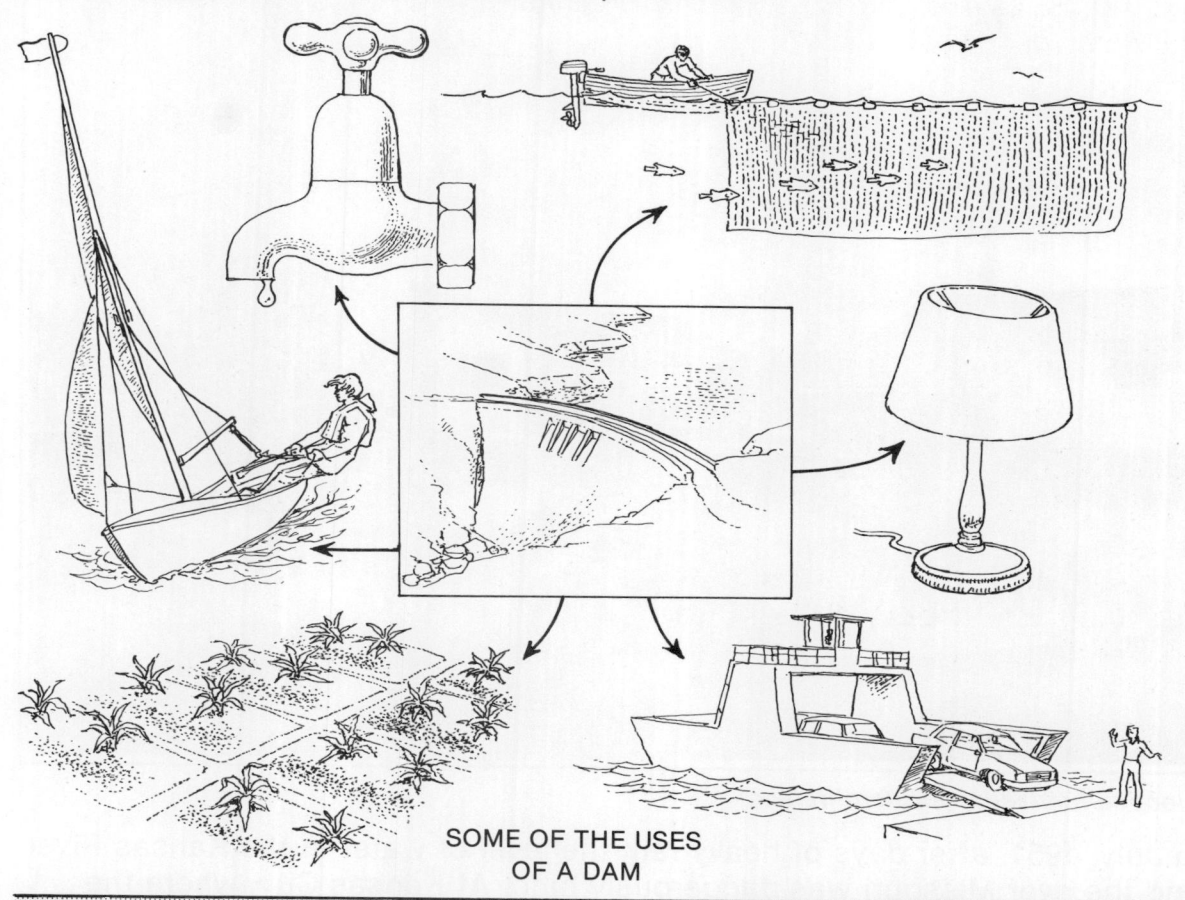

SOME OF THE USES OF A DAM

Things to do

1. Copy the diagram on this page showing some of the reasons why dams are built. Write a few words under each picture to say what is shows.

2. What happens to plants if they don't get enough water? Do humans need water?

3. Make a model of a shaduf. You will need a stick with a weight on one end and a paper bucket on the other. Hold the stick so that it rests on top of another stick and see how easy it is to swing the bucket round. The weight on one end balances the bucket of water on the other.

4. Find out where your local water comes from. Draw pictures to show how it gets to your home.

When rivers flood

Flooded homes in Northern Ireland

In July, 1951, after days of heavy rain the level of water in the Kansas River and the river Missouri was dangerously high. At Kansas City, where the two rivers joined up, the resulting floods were devastating.

Half a million people had to leave their homes and a thousand million dollars worth of damage was done. Factories, blocks of flats and offices were inundated. Photographs showed them standing in what appeared to be the middle of a huge lake.

Low-lying areas, like the Fenland in Eastern England, or the flat floors of river valleys, are at risk from floods like this. Most countries of the world have rivers which flood from time to time.

Heavy rainfall fills the rivers and causes the level to rise above the tops of the banks and so flood fields, streets and gardens. People have sometimes had to climb telegraph poles or wait on the roofs of their houses to be rescued.

marshland

farmland

There are a number of ways of trying to stop a river from flooding.

Special gates across a river, called sluice gates, can sometimes be used to control the flow of the river. They pond back the water when the tide has come up the river and open to let the water flow to the sea at low tide.

Walls of earth, called embankments, strengthen the river banks and special ditches are dug to drain away surplus water from the land. From a helicopter you might think they were irrigation channels. But instead of bringing water to the fields they take it away.

The water from these ditches is pumped into the river and allowed to flow into the sea. In the past the pumps were worked by windmills. Today oil or electricity are used. The drained land is excellent for farming, in Holland these areas are called polders.

Things to do

1. Look at the two pictures on this page. Write down three changes which took place when the area in the first picture was drained to become a polder.
2. Which parts of your town or village might flood after many days of heavy rainfall?
3. Write a few words to say how drainage channels are different from irrigation channels.

Forests

From tree to paper

This book started life as part of a pine tree!

Pine trees are those which have cones. This is why they are also called coniferous trees. Their wood is soft compared with the wood from trees which grow in tropical climates.

On these pages you can see the picture story of a tree in Canada, showing what happened to it before it was made into a roll of paper in Britain.

Coniferous forest in Canada

FROM TREE TO PAPER

A   The tree was cut down by a lumberjack in winter.

B   With other trees it was pulled by a tractor to the river bank.

C   The trees were then tipped down a shute on to the frozen river below.

D   In the spring the ice melted and the logs began to float downstream.

E When the logs bunched together and blocked the stream, a lumberjack ran across the logs and pushed away the key log, which was jamming the others back. He had to run quickly to safety before the logs surged down the river once again.

F When the logs reached the lake they were collected together and towed by a tug to the pulp mill.

G The logs were piled high outside the mill.

H Later the logs were ground down and made into pulp.

I The pulp was dried into bundles and taken by ship to Britain.

J At the factory the bundles were mixed with water to a paste and rolled and dried to become paper.

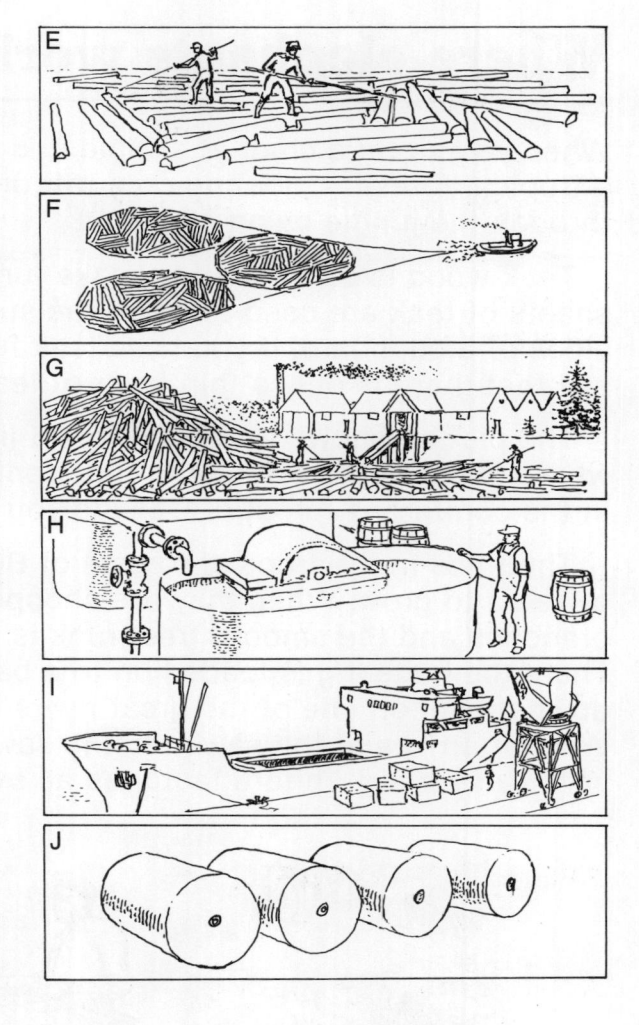

Things to do

1. Which pictures show scenes in Canada and which show scenes at a paper mill in Britain?
2. How can you tell that the weather in the coniferous forests of Canada is very cold in winter.
3. Write a few words to say what it must be like to work as a lumberjack.
4. Find out about other places in the world where wood is grown for paper. Draw a map to show these places.
5. Write a few sentences to describe how paper is made.

Where elephants work

When you sit on a chair at a table it is hard to think of it once as a tree in a tropical forest — floating on a raft on a wide river or being towed through the jungle by an elephant.

Teak wood is often used to make furniture because it is very hard. Thin sheets of teak are used to cover the surface of a table or the front and sides of a cupboard. If you have teak furniture at home you will be able to see that there is only a thin layer of teak there.

The picture shows a tropical forest in Burma, southern Asia. This is where teak trees grow. Life in this tropical forest is very different from that in the coniferous forest of Canada you read about on the previous pages.

The trees in the tropical forests of Burma are very tall and take hundreds of years to grow. When they are chopped down a worker cuts off the branches and the smooth tree trunk is then towed by elephants to a river. There the huge log is loaded on to a bamboo raft and floated slowly downstream on one of the great rivers which flow through the jungle. When it arrives at the saw mill it is sawn into planks and these are then sent by ship to furniture factories all over the world.

The weather in the tropical forests where the elephants work is hot all the year round. The trees grow tall because there is plenty of rain. It falls mainly in the summer months when the monsoon wind blows. Monsoon means season; and the monsoon weather in this part of Asia comes in the summer. There is a big difference between the summers which are hot and mainly wet and the winters when it is hot and mainly dry.

During the monsoon there are thunderstorms, torrential rains and floods. Everywhere the air feels damp. Clothes feel damp and books and papers go mouldy. The weather is so hot and wet that people who are not used to it find it a very difficult time of the year.

Things to do

1. Draw a series of six pictures, like those for the picture story 'From Tree to Paper' on pages, 52 and 53. Draw a tall tree in a tropical forest for picture A and a furniture factory for picture F. What will you show in the other pictures from B to E?
2. Write a few sentences to say how life in the coniferous forest is different from life in the tropical forest.
3. How many uses can you think of for the hard woods from the tropical forests?

Crops from trees

We normally expect a farmer to grow crops like wheat or to keep animals like sheep and cows. But some farmers grow trees instead. They grow them for their leaves, fruit, nuts, bark and sap.

Some forests are kept for their timber, as you have already seen. In Portugal and Spain the cork oak tree is grown for its bark. This is stripped from the trunk of the tree and used to make the corks you find in bottles.

Rubber trees are grown in Malaysia. The rubber comes from the sap inside the trees, which runs out when the bark of the tree is cut.

In Britain apple, pear and plum trees are grown in orchards for their fruit. In countries near the Mediterranean Sea there are olive groves where olive trees are grown. Olives are used to make oil. You will probably find a bottle of olive oil in the kitchen at home. Other trees grown in these warm countries provide almonds, dates, figs, apricots and peaches. Vineyards are places where grapes are grown on vines. Most of the grapes are crushed and made into wine, but some are dried to make raisins, currants and sultanas.

Top to bottom:
Oranges
A banana grove
Pineapple; Cocoa pods
Picking lychee nuts in Hong Kong

In tropical countries, like those of the Caribbean Sea or Central America, citrus fruits are grown such as lemons, oranges and grapefruit. Other crops from trees include coconuts and bananas.

Large farms, where trees are grown from seed and planted in rows, are called plantations. In India, Ceylon and China tea bushes are grown. During the growing season the workers on the plantations pick the leaves of the tea bush and put them in a sack. The leaves are taken to a factory where they are dried and crushed to make the small bits of tea you can see in a tea bag or in a packet of tea.

In Kenya and Brazil there are coffee plantations where the coffee cherries are picked and crushed to remove the beans inside. These are dried and roasted to become coffee.

In Ghana, Africa, cocoa trees are grown on plantations and the cocoa pods picked in October, November and December. Inside each pod there are over thirty cocoa beans which are dried, and then sold to be made into chocolate.

Things to do

1. What crops from trees can be found in your home? Make a list of them and collect labels, wrappers and adverts which say where the crops were grown.
2. Write a few words to explain what is meant by
   1) a plantation
   2) an orchard
   3) an olive grove
   4) a vineyard
   5) citrus fruits

Grasslands

Land of tall grass

Savanna grassland

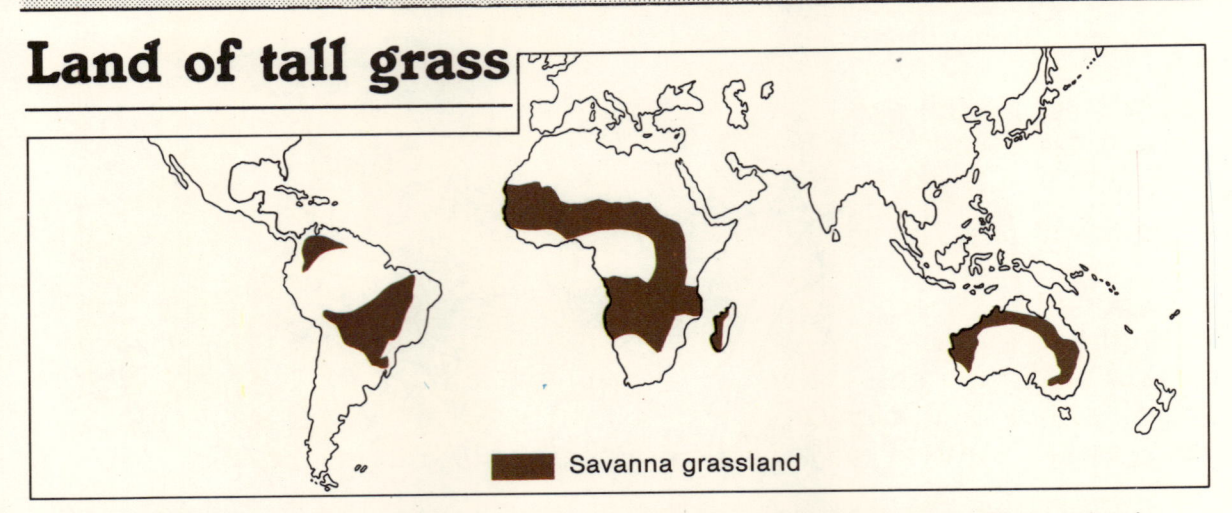

Imagine a trip in the school bus shown in the picture below. These lucky African children are on a visit to a game reserve or national park. This is a large area of tropical grassland which has been set aside as a place where wild animals can live without fear of being hunted by humans. This tropical grassland is sometimes called the savanna.

On their school visit the children see antelopes, gazelles, hartebeestes and eland grazing by a waterhole, whilst further on lions and cheetahs stalk their prey.

The children discover that the savanna contains many trees as well as grassland. Among the clumps of trees and in the tall yellow grass, the children see zebras, a rhinoceros, several elephants, impala and a number of giraffes.

A game warden tells them that the reason why so many different wild animals can live here is because most of them eat different foods. The giraffes eat leaves from trees, whilst antelopes eat grass and lions eat antelopes.

Water is usually a problem in the savanna. There are only a few rivers and waterholes. Many animals go in herds to drink at these waterholes; some drink their fill of water whilst the others keep watch for hunting animals like the lion and the leopard. Some animals drink at night and others during the day.

The weather is hot and dry for much of the year, so the grass withers and changes colour and the soil turns to fine dust. Herdsmen have to drive their cattle long distances in search of good grass and plentiful water.

For the rest of the year the weather is hot and wet. The grassland recovers and the tall yellow grass provides good grazing for the animals.

Things to do

1. See if you can find out the answers to these questions.
   1) Which animals are usually only found on the open grassland?
   2) Which animals are sometimes found in the woodland areas?
   3) Why does the giraffe feed from the high branches of a tree?
   4) What do lions, cheetahs and hyenas feed on?
   5) Why do giraffes, antelopes and other animals keep together in herds?

2. Write a few sentences to describe the savanna grasslands of Africa.

3. Find out which of the animals living in the savanna lands have been in danger of becoming extinct. Explain why this is and how they are protected nowadays.

Land of short grass

The next time you watch an American cowboy film, look closely at the prairies where the cowboys ride. Much of this land is flat and monotonous with short grassland and very few trees. Trees like plenty of moisture and the prairies are fairly dry, with rain falling mainly in the summer months.

The first people to live here were the Indians who hunted the bison that roamed the grassy plains. Then white people came and there was conflict. They killed off the bison and grazed large herds of cattle instead.

Not long afterwards, when the railways were built, farmers came from other parts of America and from Europe to grow crops. They often quarrelled with the cattle ranchers.

The prairies seemed ideal for corn growing since they were flat and fertile, and could be divided into large fields, which made it easier to use machinery. The weather, which was very hot in summer, made the corn ripen quickly.

But there were disadvantages as well. The weather was bitterly cold in winter and sometimes there were long periods of drought.

Today wheat and barley are grown mainly in the eastern half of the prairies where there is more rainfall. The cattle are reared on large ranches in the west. The cowboys still ride horses but nowadays drive tractors as well.

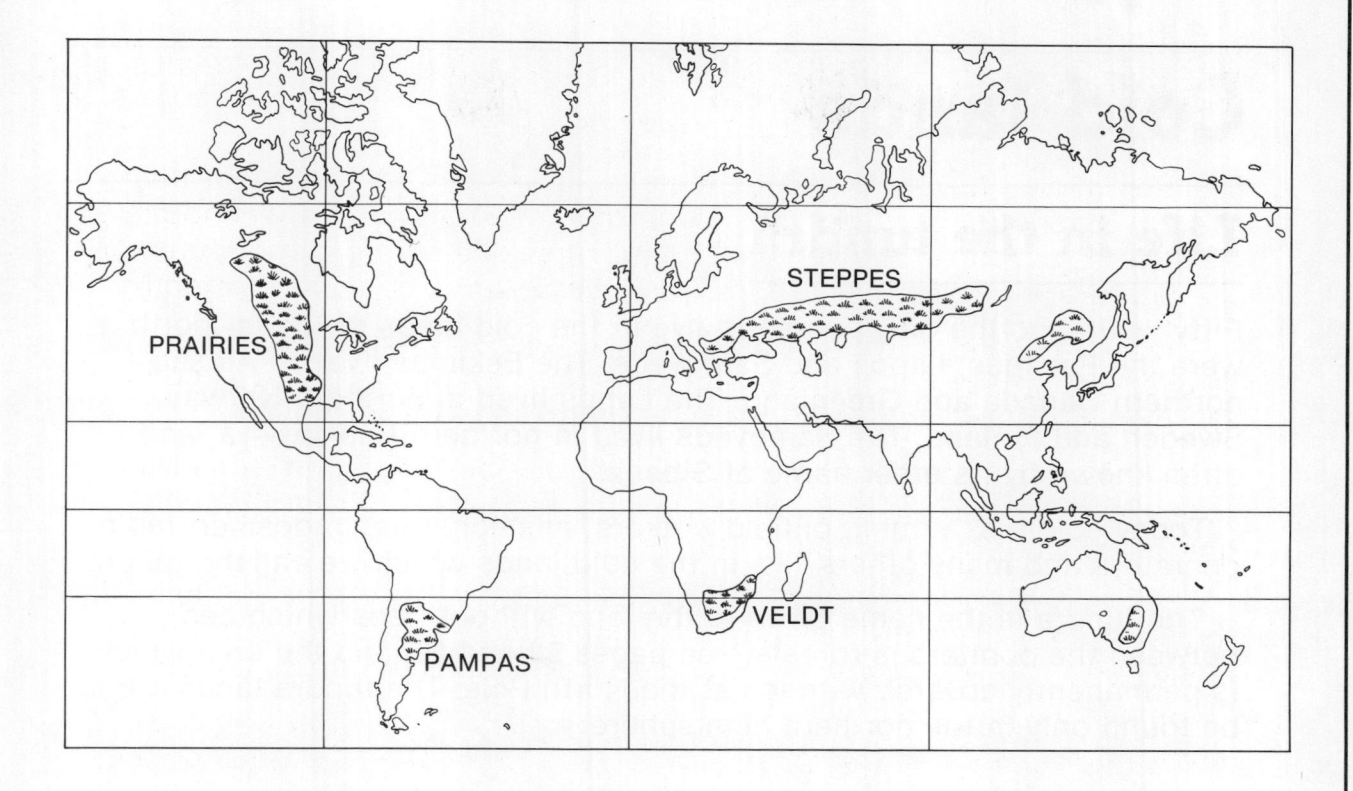

Lands like this can be seen in other parts of the world. In Russia the short grasslands are called the steppes, where they are used to grow corn and rear animals. Much of the world's flour and meat comes from the prairies of North America and the steppes of Russia.

In South America the prairies are called the pampas, the cowboys are gauchos and the ranches, estancias. In South Africa the short grassland is known as the veldt. On similar land in Australia merino sheep are reared on large sheep stations for their thick wool.

Things to do

1. Make a list of the advantages of the prairies for growing corn. What are the disadvantages?

2. Look at the map showing the prairies, steppes, veldt and pampas. What have all these areas of short grassland got in common?

3. Write a few sentences to explain how the weather in the prairies differs from the weather you have at home.

4. Explain the meaning of the following words
    1) prairies   3) steppes   5) gauchos   7) veldt
    2) bison   4) pampas   6) estancias

Cold lands

Life in the tundra

Fifty years ago the only people to live in the cold lands of the far north were the Eskimos, Lapps and Samoyeds. The Eskimos lived in Alaska, northern Canada and Greenland. The Lapps lived in northern Norway, Sweden and Finland. The Samoyeds lived in northern Russia — a land often known by its other name of Siberia.

Today soldiers, airmen, oilfield workers, missionaries, tradesmen, radio operators and many others live in the cold lands which we call the tundra.

The tundra is the name given to the land without trees which lies between the coniferous forests, see pages 52 and 53, and the area which is permanently covered with ice at the North Pole. The tundra lands are to be found only in the northern hemisphere.

JANUARY—FEBRUARY
depths of winter

MARCH—APRIL
still winter but days are getting lighter

MAY
snow and ice start to melt — caribou come north from the coniferous forests

JUNE
lakes and rivers full of water

JULY
daylight at midnight — quite warm — many insects and mosquitoes

AUGUST
flowers carpet the ground but the days are cooler

SEPTEMBER
first snowstorms — the caribou go back to the forests

OCTOBER–NOVEMBER–DECEMBER
winter once more — days getting darker

For most of the year the tundra is covered with ice and snow, as you can see from the pictures on these pages which show a year at the tundra.

For a very brief time in the summer months, the snow melts and the lands are bright with flowers. Then the cold weather returns and the ground freezes and is covered with snow.

Eskimos, Lapps and Samoyeds still live in these lands but their life has changed. Many of the goods we enjoy, such as radio, television, motor vehicles, electric cookers and modern foods are on sale in these lands. Oil has been discovered in Alaska, iron ore is mined in northern Canada, coal and other minerals are taken from the tundra lands of Europe and Russia. So there are new jobs for the people who live there besides fishing and hunting seals and reindeer.

Things to do

1. Look at the pictures. How long is the winter in the tundra? How long is the summer? How does the summer differ from the winter?
2. Write a number of sentences to say how a year at the tundra differs from a year in the place where you live.

Index

Abbreviations 5
Arabs 30–31
Ash (volcanic) 34–37
Atlases 14–15

Beaches 27–29
Bedouin 31

Camels 31
Cliff features 28–29
Coasts 26–29
Compass directions 11
Coniferous forests 7, 52–53
Cowboys and Indians 60–61

Dams 48–49
Deserts 30–33
Directions 10–11
Drainage 51
Drawing a map 12–13
Drought 46

Earth rotation 16–17
Earthquakes 36–39
Equator 17

Finding your way 10–11
Fishing 27
Flooding 18–19, 26, 44, 50–51
Fold mountains 24–25

Forestry 25, 52–55
Gazetteer 14
Globe 16–17
Grasslands 58–61

Holidays 25, 27
Hydro-electricity 49

Ice 22–24, 42, 62–63
Irrigation 46–49

Map directions 10–11
Map-drawing 12–13
Map references 6–7
Map scales 8–9
Map symbols 4–5
Monsoon 55
Mountains 22–25

North Pole 17

Oasis 33
Oil 31
Orchards 56–57

Paper-making 52–53
Plantations 56–57
Ports 27
Prairies 60–61
Pulp and paper 52–53

Rain 50
Reservoir 48–49
Resorts 25, 27
Rivers 18–21, 50–51
Rocks 40–43
Rotation of earth 16–17

Savanna 58–59
Scale maps 8–9
Sea 26–29
Sheep farming 25
Sketch-maps 12–13
Snow 22–24, 62–63
Soil erosion 44–45
Soils 42–43
South Pole 17
Symbols 4–5

Teak forests 54–55
Tree crops 56–57
Tropical forests 54–55
Tropical grasslands 58–59
Tropics 17, 20–21, 54–55, 58–59
Tundra 62–63

Volcanoes 34–37, 39–40

Wadis 32
Water supplies 49–49, 59
Wave action 28–29

Acknowledgements

Designed by Visual Art Productions
Illustrations by V.A.P. Group and Gay Galsworthy
The authors and publishers wish to acknowledge the following photograph sources:

Cover	Jim Brownbill		
Page 25	Philip Sauvain	Page 52	Popperfoto
Page 26 & 29	John Topham Picture Library	Page 56	John Topham Picture Library
Page 29	British Tourist Authority		Valerie Randall
Page 38	John Topham Picture Library		Professor Don Tindall
Pages 40, 41 & 46	Philip Sauvain		U.A.C. Ltd
			Hong Kong Information Service
Page 50	J. Allan Cash	Page 60	U.S. Information Service

The publishers have made every effort to trace the copyright owners, but where they have failed to do so they will be pleased to make the necessary arrangements at the first opportunity.

Text © Philip Sauvain
Illustrations © Macmillan Education Ltd 1983

All rights reserved. No reproduction, copy or transmission of this publication may be made without written permission.

No paragraph of this publication may be reproduced, copied or transmitted save with written permission or in accordance with the provisions of the Copyright Act 1956 (as amended).

Any person who does any unauthorised act in relation to this publication may be liable to criminal prosecution and civil claims for damages.

First published 1983
Reprinted 1985

Published by
MACMILLAN EDUCATION LTD
Houndmills, Basingstoke, Hampshire RG21 2XS
and London
Companies and representatives
throughout the world

Printed in Hong Kong

ISBN 0–333–31145–0